The
SuperNatural
HABITS
of the
SPIRIT-EMPOWERED
BELIEVER

by Paul & Nuala O'Higgins

The Supernatural Habits of the Spirit-Empowered Believer
Copyrights © 2016 Paul & Nuala O'Higgins

3rd Edition 2016
ISBN-13: 978-1482500714
ISBN-10: 148250071X

Published by Reconciliation Outreach Inc.
P.O. Box 2778, Stuart, FL 34995
www.reconciliationoutreach.net

Category: Christian, Inspiration

ACKNOWLEDGEMENTS

Our special thanks go to our friends and fellow students at THE 120 CLUB at Ft. Pierce and Stuart, Florida who encouraged us to write this book and to Sean O'Healy for his invaluable help in editing.

CONTENTS

INTRODUCTION

This book is not a formula for discovering your possibilities and maximizing your potential.

It is not about developing your possibilities - it is about developing your impossibilities. It is about living a life that we are totally incapable of living, other than by the supernatural power of the Holy Spirit.

The tragedy of the human condition is that we are naturally incapable of living the life we want to live and know we should live. The paradox of the moral life is that, as Paul so well expressed it, *"the good I want to do I don't, and the evil I don't want to do, I do."* (Romans 7:19) What misery! We are invisibly chained with bonds that hinder us from living the life of love, joy and faith we know we are destined for.

By the gift of the Holy Spirit – Christ Jesus living in us - we can be released from these chains, which are the power of sin. The solution to the law of sin is the law and life of the Spirit. This is God's great solution to man's moral problem.

"For I delight in the law of God after the inward man: but I see a different law in my members, warring against the law of my mind, and bringing me into captivity under the law of sin which is in my members. Wretched man that I am! Who shall deliver me out of the body of this death? I thank God through Jesus Christ our Lord. So then I of myself with the mind, indeed, serve the law of God; but with the flesh the law of sin."

"There is therefore now no condemnation to them that are in Christ Jesus. For the law of the Spirit of life in Christ Jesus made me free from the law of sin and of death." (Romans 7:22 - 8:2)

This life of the Spirit creates the possibility of a whole new set of moral habits for us, which were previously beyond our reach. It is these habits we explore in this book. That which was once impossible is now possible. That which was once unnatural to us becomes supernaturally natural.

The prophets realized God's high standard, and man's failure to live by it. As they wrestled with this problem, God showed them He would solve the problem by making a new covenant with them and by putting His Spirit within them.

"Behold, the days come, says the LORD, that I will cut a new covenant with the house of Israel, and with the house of Judah, not according to the covenant that I cut with their fathers in the day I took them by the hand to bring them out of the land of Egypt; which covenant of Mine they broke, although I was a husband to them, says the LORD; But this shall be the covenant that I will cut with the house of Israel: After those days, says the LORD, I will put My law in their inward parts, and write it in their hearts; and I will be their God, and they shall be My people." (Jeremiah 31:31-33)

Here, God promises to take out the hard heart we possess that makes spiritual living impossible and replace it with a new tender heart. *"And I will give you a new heart, and I will put a new spirit within you. And I will take away the stony heart out of your flesh, and I will give you a heart of flesh."* (Ezekiel 36:26) God will so transform us that by the Spirit we can be empowered to walk in His ways and live by a new set of standards and habits.

Self-help books are directed to the will of man. The habits in this book are possible only as we are empowered from a dimension greater than willpower - the Holy Spirit.

When we recognize the bankruptcy of the merely natural man we can place our faith in something greater than ourselves - the life of the One who has come to live within us. As we do this we draw from the life of the Spirit.

This life is available to all who by faith reach out beyond themselves to the life of Jesus. As Isaiah 12:3 puts it: *"with joy you will draw water from the wells of Salvation (Jesus)"* i.e. we will learn to draw spiritual strength from a Source beyond ourselves.

And as Jesus Himself says: *"I am the Vine, you are the branches. He who abides in Me, and I in him, the same brings forth much fruit; for without Me you can do nothing."* (John 15:5)

Discipline is required, of course. But it is not the kind of discipline that pushes us to do what we cannot do. It is the discipline of constantly drawing from the Holy Spirit who empowers us to do what was previously impossible to us. It is the discipline of those who know that *"without faith it is impossible to please God."* (Hebrews 11.6)

One of the great lacks of much of contemporary Christianity is that it distorts the work of the New Covenant by pointing to the remission of sin without pointing to the removal from sin's power. The New Covenant is the remission of sin through the death and resurrection of Jesus and it is also the empowerment to live at a supernatural level of moral and spiritual excellence through the power of the Spirit.

Christian living is held together by two paradoxical sayings:

- *"I can do nothing of my own"* and
- *"I can do all things through Him who strengthens me."*

Psychology is directed to harnessing the powers of the natural man. Christianity, on the other hand, harnesses the power of supernatural life. This can be discovered and experienced by those who are profoundly aware of the weakness of the natural man and receive the supernatural power of the Holy Spirit to empower them for a life of love and joy. It is here that real Christianity is so superior to humanism. It fulfills the goal of the humanist by drawing not on natural human life but on the life of Another.

The revelation of the prophets and the apostles is that moral life cannot be lived apart from the presence of the Spirit of God within us. Without Him this life is impossible, but with Him it becomes supernaturally natural.

This book is an introduction to the supernatural habits of the Spirit-filled believer. Though this life is natural it is not automatic, as we must learn to function with our new "wings", put off the old ways and put on the ways of the Spirit.

It is not an attempt not to exalt the powers of human goodness but to discover once again the life at the reverse side of human failure.

CHAPTER 1

THE HABIT OF THANKSGIVING

The first habit that we will look at is the habit of thanksgiving.

It is the most basic habit of the believer. It is the heart's response to the reality of God's love and mercy.

The most supernaturally empowered believers are the greatest rejoicers, praisers and thanksgivers. *"Rejoice in the Lord always, again I say rejoice."* (Philippians 4:4) They bring non-stop thanksgiving to God to whom they owe everything and from whom they receive everything. Thanksgiving is the heart's automatic reaction to the happy reality of the kingdom of God.

THANK WHOM?

Thanksgiving is not just a positive attitude practiced by optimists – it is an acknowledgment that we are the beneficiaries of somebody else's goodness and help.

The atheist can be thankful, but he cannot be thankful to God.

Thanksgiving is the attitude of those who recognize that all that we have, and are, are gifts from God and that we owe Him thanks for everything.

Thanksgiving is worship. Through it we acknowledge God and our debt to Him.

Through it we develop the relationship of love He destined us for.

"Hear, O Israel, the Lord your God the Lord is one, thou shall love the Lord with all your heart, with all your soul, with all your strength." (Deut. 6:4)

Thanksgiving is our acknowledgment as created beings that we are indebted to our Creator.

"The fear of the Lord is the beginning of wisdom." (Psalm 111.10) The beginning of all right, wise and effective living is to acknowledge God. He can do perfectly well without us, but we would neither exist nor remain in existence without Him.

"Every good endowment and every perfect gift is from above, coming down from the Father of lights with whom there is no variation or shadow due to change." (James 1:17)

Because everything I have and am is a gift from God, thanksgiving is the natural response to this reality. Thanksgiving is simply the realistic and humble acknowledgment we give to God for our creation and redemption. Scripture says that

God created and *"destined us in love to be his sons through Jesus Christ, according to the purpose of his will, to the praise of his glorious grace which he freely bestowed on us in the Beloved."* (Ephesians 1:5-6)

We were created to give thanks as surely as birds were made to sing their songs. They sing by compulsion – it's their nature to sing. We give thanks by choice. Thanking God for His grace is an essential part of our destiny. Since we were created to give thanks, we function at our best and most effectively when we do give thanks. Supernaturally empowered believers learn to live a lifestyle of praise and thanksgiving. By doing this they are simply fulfilling their destiny.

THANKS FOR WHAT?

As believers we thank God not only for our existence - the gift of life and all that supports life - but above all we thank Him for our redemption. We thank Him for the great salvation that has come to us through the cross and resurrection of Jesus.

"If Christ is not risen from the dead, then our preaching is empty and your faith is also empty." (1 Corinthians 15:14) If there is no resurrection

and redemption then there is no eternal life for us. Life for all of us would end in eternal death and destruction. But because Jesus has died for our sins (and we believe it) we know we have eternal life and will live forever in the Father's love and blessing here on earth and throughout all ages!

God has reconciled us to Himself, given us all things, and continues to supply our every need. Thankfulness to God is the basis of real faith and increase.

We thank God for life, for redemption, for Jesus and His work for us, for the covenant we have with Him, for the destiny He has given us and for His Fatherly care in everything. *"In everything give thanks for this is the will of God in Christ Jesus concerning you."* (1 Thess. 5:18)

The Redemption - the work that Jesus did for us by His cross, resurrection and ascension - is the basis of the believer's thanksgiving. This is what separates the thanksgiving of believers from all other kinds of thanksgiving. It is not simply a polite acknowledgment of a benefit received. It is an act by which we return our lives to their true center. Thanksgiving is related to the atonement in a special way. We thank God that:

- our sins are atoned through Jesus and we are reconciled to God

- the curse has been removed and sin and oppression have lost their dominion over us

- we have received the Holy Spirit

- we are new creations, and adopted sons of God

- we are commissioned and equipped to go into the world as He went into the world, and

- because of Jesus, we are blessed with every spiritual blessing, and our whole life is in covenant relationship with God and with His keeping power.

Throughout all eternity we will be thanking God for the blood of Jesus the Lamb who has taken away the sins of the world.

We are eternally indebted to Him, eternally grateful to Him and eternally appreciative of this awesome gift. We certainly did not deserve this amazing grace – we can only acknowledge it with thanksgiving and humble gratitude.

This thanksgiving for creation and redemption separates the believer's thanksgiving from the mere positive thinking of psychology. It is the basis of all faith. *"Without faith it is impossible to please God; for whoever comes to Him must believe that God EXISTS and is the REWARDER of those who diligently seek Him."* (Heb. 11:6)

Thanksgiving is simply our faith acknowledging reality. By it we orient ourselves correctly to the Source of all reality. The more we cultivate gratitude for our redemption and for Him as a person the more we will experience His love and the more our hearts will be aligned to Him and His way.

SACRIFICE OF PRAISE

With thanksgiving we recall and remember Jesus' once-for-all sacrifice for us, and as we do this we activate its reality afresh in our lives. *"Through him then let us continually offer up a sacrifice of praise to God, that is, the fruit of lips that acknowledge his name."* (Hebrews 13:15)

Since Christ has died for our sins, there remains no more sacrifice for sin except the sacrifice of praise (thanksgiving) by which we acknowledge and appropriate the blessings God has provided.

This is why the communion service of the church is often called "Eucharist" or "Thanksgiving Service". The communion service is one of the ways we offer the sacrifice of praise for the once-for-all sacrifice. Here we take bread and wine to recall the death and resurrection of Jesus, His atonement for us, as an act of thanks. As we give thanks for this amazing gift we activate and appropriate its benefits afresh. To remember and give thanks 'worthily' is to give thanks, consciously realizing and remembering the meaning and effects of what He has done for us.

THANKING GOD FOR ALL HIS BENEFITS

"Oh give thanks to the Lord for he is good for his mercies endure forever". (Ps. 107:1)

This was the great song of the priests in the Temple days and is the great praise of believers of all generations.

"Give thanks to the Lord for his mercies are new every morning." (Lamentations 3.23)

"Give thanks to the Lord who daily loads us with benefits." (Ps. 68:19)

"With joy you will draw water from the wells of salvation." (Isa. 12:3)

Through thanksgiving for the atoning sacrifice we approach God and receive His mercies at all our points of need. Through it we recognize that nothing we are or have is due to us alone. It is only through His mercy that we continue to exist and it is only through His mercy that we are sustained spiritually, morally and physically.

THANKSGIVING & PRIDE

Pride is the attitude of not acknowledging or not receiving God's mercies.

Presumption is the attitude of not recognizing our need of His mercies. Failure to thank is, therefore, an expression of both presumption and pride.

Pride is the root of all sin and the source of all separation from God and His care. Thanksgiving is the perfect antidote to pride, because it keeps us in the position of acknowledging, celebrating and continuously receiving God's mercies.

As priests of the Most High God, it is our happy and glorious responsibility to thank Him in everything, and for everything.

Believers are members of 'The Perpetual Celebration Society' because they are people who continually give thanks.

With thanksgiving we acknowledge and draw to ourselves all the mercies God makes available to us in His promises. Through it we also position ourselves to continue in the benefits He has already given us. Every breath we take, every quality of spiritual, physical, intellectual and moral health is a gift from Him. Every blessing and ability to bless others is a gift from Him. If He were to withdraw His mercies we would cease to function spiritually, mentally, morally and financially. Through thanksgiving we acknowledge that indeed all these blessings are expressions of His mercy and not of our ingenuity. The supernaturally empowered believer never ceases to ask God to have mercy on him and to never withdraw His mercies from him.

"Have mercy on me Lord and take not your Holy Spirit from me." (Psalm 51) If He should withdraw His hand and mercy from us we would collapse in every way.

Veteran Bible Teacher Arthur Burt recalls that, during The Second World War, when he was working as an evangelist, he persistently refused the military draft. In 1943 he was brought before a tribunal in London where they mocked and ridiculed him. "I believe God has given me a word to be what I am, where I am", he explained to them.

'Oh so you have a golden telephone and are in touch with the Almighty?' they mocked, 'We'll see about that!' Then they sentenced him to prison for contempt of court!

While in prison he became irritated with one of the other prisoners who was a chronic smoker. The smoker continually asked Arthur to give him his ration of cigarettes for which Arthur had no use. "One day", Arthur recalls, "he irritated me so much I just blew my top. I was wrong but I shouted 'Shut up and leave me alone!'"

Then God dealt with Arthur: "How dare you speak to that man like that. You are no different. You are just like him and you smoke like a chimney."

"But Lord, I don't smoke," Arthur objected.

"Yes you do," he corrected, "what keeps you from smoking is my grace. If I remove my grace, you will be exactly as bad as that man. It is my grace in you that has delivered you from the habit. Don't attribute to your character that which is a work of my grace."

Arthur learnt in a deep way that we are all completely sinful apart from God's keeping mercy. Our spiritual, moral and physical health (even when we don't recognize it) would crumble to ruin apart from His presence. The supernaturally empowered believer knows that he owes everything he has, and is, to Someone who deserves his constant thanks and recognition.

THANKSGIVING BRINGS INCREASE

One of the greatest miracles in the gospels is the healing of ten lepers by Jesus. Nothing like this had ever happened since time began. After He healed them He told them to go to the Temple and show themselves to the priest so that they could be accepted back in Jewish society. All ten went on their way rejoicing but only one came back to give thanks for the miracle. The one who returned received a second miracle - he was "made whole".

The parts of his body that the leprosy had eaten were restored in a creative miracle (Lk. 17:12-19).

> He who flows in thanksgiving recognizes that he is swimming in a sea of God's mercies.

When we give thanks and acknowledge what we have received we actually open our hearts to receive even more. *"To him who has will more be given and he will have abundance."* (Matthew 13:12

THANK OTHERS

Supernaturally empowered believers not only acknowledge God with thanks but also acknowledge all the channels God uses to bless and help them. This is why it is only reasonable that we thank God not only for what He has given to us directly but for all the people He has used to help us: parents, educators, school friends, mentors, pastors, preachers, doctors, maintenance men - the thousands of people who have formed a human chain to cause us to be alive today. As for me, even the bread on my table today, the shirt on my back and the home I live in have come to me through a complex matrix of services and planners, from manufacturing systems, agricultural systems, transportation systems, banking systems and political systems that involve literally millions of people. I am aware that the fact) that I am writing on this computer, sitting on this chair, in my home, is the result of a network of services and people that form a human chain that enable me to do what I am doing today. "No man is an island .... each man is part of the main" (John Donne, "No Man is an Island"). Failure to acknowledge our debt to other humans is sheer blindness and is the epitome of arrogance. How much we take for granted!

Without the habit of thanksgiving we act as if everything were our right, and we complain like spoiled children. The truth is that we are debtors to everyone. It is not possible to thank everyone for everything or to even notice everything that everyone does for us. The person who flows in thanksgiving and humility recognizes that he is swimming in a sea of God's mercies. These mercies come to us directly from God and indirectly through hosts of people. Acknowledging people with thanks and recognition relates us to them in a healthy and right way.

THANKING GOD FOR ALL MEN

"First of all, then, I urge that supplications, prayers, intercessions and thanksgivings be made for all men, for kings and all who are in high positions,

that we may lead a quiet and peaceable life, Godly and respectful in every way." (1 Timothy 2:1-2)

We can't begin to pray until we begin to acknowledge our linkage and debt to all human beings. We are debtors to all men and so we thank God for every one of them and recognize our debt to them. We do not agree with everything that everyone does but we know that God uses everything and everyone for our good when we acknowledge Him.

Unthankfulness is the breeding ground for negativity. It is the gateway for discouragement, self-pity, unforgiveness, bitterness, frustration, envy, and covetousness.

Unthankfulness is like a shade we pull down that shuts out the sunlight and leaves us in the darkness of self-absorption, selfishness and self-pity.

Thankfulness, on the other hand, is like pulling back a curtain, which opens a window to the goodness and blessings of God and to all that is positive and good.

"Finally, brethren, whatever is true, whatever is honorable, whatever is just, whatever is pure, whatever is lovely, whatever is gracious, if there is any excellence, if there is anything worthy of praise, think about these things." (Phil. 4:8)

'Two men looked out through prison bars, the one saw mud and the other stars' (Dale Carnegie).

In spite of all the suffering, evil and injustice that exist in this world we recognize that *"the earth is full of the mercy of the Lord."* (Ps. 33:5) The most supernaturally empowered believer, while conscious of the suffering and evil in the world, never loses sight of this great fact and constantly remains attuned to it. Thanksgiving is simply a part of the life of faith. By it we acknowledge God's goodness as it comes to us in so many forms.

"Blessed be the Lord, who daily loads us with benefits, even the God of our salvation. Selah." (Ps. 68:19) Faith acknowledges through thanksgiving that we are loaded with God's benefits and it opens us for more of His benefits.

THE HEALING POWER OF THANKSGIVING

There is tremendous healing power in thanksgiving. Those with a thankful heart live longer, get sick less and enjoy life more.

"A merry heart does well like a medicine, but a broken spirit dries the bones." (Proverbs 17:22)

"A merry heart makes a cheerful countenance: but by sorrow of the heart the spirit is broken." (Proverbs 15:13)

The scriptures attribute amazing healing benefits to the attitude of thankfulness and cheerfulness. Cheerfulness is said to be equivalent to a good medicine.

Medical science substantiates this. People who have a cheerful disposition tend to live longer and enjoy long years. Modern physiology shows that cheerfulness causes the release of dopamine and a reduction in cortisol. Excess cortisol damages the arteries, suppresses the immune system and inhibits sleep.

Proverbs tells us that, when our hearts are not cheerful and are broken, our bones are dried up. What is it to have dried up bones?

The 'wet' part of the bone is the bone marrow, which of course is one of the most important parts of the immune system. It is the marrow that produces the white blood cells, which fight off fungal infections, parasites and cancer cells. With a depressed bone marrow the body's ability to fight off disease is greatly reduced.

Depression, sorrow and grief, according to the Bible, dry the bones i.e. inhibit the bone marrow, and so cause all sorts of diseases. The merry heart, or the spirit of thanksgiving, is the antidote for this. Jesus came *'to heal the broken hearted'* and *'to give us the garment of praise for the spirit of heaviness.'* (Isaiah 61:3, Luke 4.18)

Since the Fall, a pall of sorrow, depression and heaviness has fallen over mankind. The earth is full of pain, suffering, sorrow and heartbreak. The great news is that Jesus took these sorrows, pains and grieves upon Himself. We can, therefore, release them to Him by faith and receive the healing oil of joy. He came to make that exchange. He was a man of sorrows because He took ours upon Himself. He became sorrowful for a moment on Calvary that we might become joyful with Him forever. He came, as Isaiah saw, *"to give them beauty for ashes, the oil of joy for mourning, the mantle of praise for the spirit of heaviness"* (Isaiah 61:3)

Through thankful remembrance we draw this joy and all the other benefits of our redemption to ourselves.

Joy is a fruit of the Spirit. The Holy Spirit generates it within us. When we are in union with Jesus, we are in union with the Spirit of joy. Through faith we receive the Holy Spirit and are filled with the Spirit. But we cannot maintain our filling without cultivating the habit of thanksgiving. Many who have been filled with the Holy Spirit lose the joy of their experience and the Spirit-filled life because they do not maintain the habit of joyful thanksgiving.

"Therefore do not be foolish, but understand what the will of the Lord is. And do not get drunk with wine, for that is debauchery; but be filled with the Spirit, addressing one another in psalms and hymns and spiritual songs, singing and making melody to the Lord with all your heart, always and for everything giving thanks in the name of our Lord Jesus Christ to God the Father." (Ephesians 5:17-20)

THANKSGIVING IS PRO-ACTIVE

Some believers believe and act as if the more solemn and joyless they are the more spiritual they are. They think that it is their duty, in light of the problems of the world, to be somber, dour and grave. This is not what God teaches. He calls us to a life of joy and celebration in the face of difficulties.

> The unthankful heart ... discovers no mercies; but let the thankful heart sweep through the day and, as the magnet finds the iron, so it will find, in every hour, some heavenly blessings!
> – Henry Ward Beecher

As Nehemiah said in the face of tremendous problems *"the joy of the Lord is your strength."* (Neh. 8:10)

To cultivate this spirit is one of the great keys to remaining in union with God and to overcome the world.

To live in thanksgiving and joy is not to be like Pollyanna, unconcerned with the problems of the world, or irresponsible about our own. It is simply refusing to be dragged down by events around us that we face. Thanksgiving gives us the ability to continue to recognize that God's resources are sufficient to meet every problem. Sometimes His resources give us the power to remove problems. Sometimes they give us the power to endure problems and sometimes they give us the power to overcome problems. Whichever way it is, His grace is sufficient for every situation we can ever find ourselves in. *"And He said to me, 'My grace is sufficient for you, for My power is made perfect in weakness.' Most gladly therefore I will rather glory in my weaknesses, that the power of Christ may overshadow me."* (2 Cor. 12:9)

The spirit of thanksgiving empowers us to use every difficulty as an opportunity to receive God's help, which is always sufficient to make all situations work for our good and to turn even the most unpleasant situation into an opportunity and a stepping stone. This is no mere positive thinking.

This is the positive reality of God's loving presence available to those who lean on Him.

Even in times of trial and darkness we can thank Him because His grace is still available to get us through and to make the negative experience work for our good. We thank God in everything and for everything He does to redeem all situations.

When we love God and invite Him into our situations He takes every circumstance - the good and the bad, the just and the unjust, the things that should not have happened as well as the things that should have happened - and makes them all work together for our good. In this way we can live without regret about the past or the present, or without fear of the future, because as Paul says, *"We know that in everything God works for good with those who love him, who are called according to his purpose."* (Romans 8:28)

Thanksgiving is not a denial of problems. On the contrary it gives us the power to do something about them, and to pro-act. As we do this we begin to embrace and experience God's redemptive ability to bring good out of evil and to make all things work together for our good. By thanksgiving we overcome victoriously rather than descend into despair.

> The supernaturally empowered believer makes his life a complaint free zone

Corrie ten Boom, the famous Christian holocaust survivor, recalled how in their horrible camp the situation became even worse when an infestation of lice broke out.

When Corrie began to murmur, her sister Betsy (who did not survive the camp) corrected Corrie and told her that she must thank God for the lice and not complain! They began to thank God for the lice that in some way God would use them for their good. Betsy and Corrie conducted Bible studies for their fellow prisoners and because of the lice the prison guards did not inspect their area. They were left to conduct their Bible studies with freedom – all because of the lice!

THANKSGIVING KEEPS US FILLED WITH THE SPIRIT

"Therefore do not be foolish, but understand what the will of the Lord is. And do not get drunk with wine, for that is debauchery; but be filled with the Spirit, addressing one another in psalms and hymns and spiritual songs, singing and making melody to the Lord with all your heart, always and for everything giving thanks in the name of our Lord Jesus Christ to God the Father." (Ephes. 5: 17-20)

As we cultivate this habit of rejoicing in the Lord and thanking God the Father through Jesus, we cause the life of the Spirit to bubble up within us.

> Who does not thank for little will not thank for much. – Estonian Proverb

Often believers, who are filled and baptized with the Holy Spirit, become flat in their faith and the vibrancy of their relationship with God begins to wane The habit of thanksgiving is the antidote to this. Our emotions sometimes pick up the heaviness of the world around us and this can quench the life of the Spirit in us. As we remind ourselves of the Lord's presence, faithfulness and goodness, we can stir ourselves up, overcome the spirit of the world around us and be restored to the joy of the Lord.

David says, *"Restore to me the joy of my salvation and renew a right spirit in me."* (Psalm 51:10) Thanksgiving restores the Spirit's life, presence and fruit to our lives and is the great key to the enjoyment of everything. *"I will offer to you the sacrifice of thanksgiving, and will call on the name of the LORD."* (Psalm 116:17) It often takes an effort of will to begin to give thanks. This is one of the reasons it is called 'the sacrifice of thanksgiving' but as we offer this sacrifice our joy will be restored and our spirit re-ignited.

THANKSGIVING SANCTIFIES EVERYTHING

"For everything created by God is good, and nothing is to be rejected if it is received with thanksgiving; for then it is consecrated by the Word of God and prayer." (1 Timothy 4:4-5)

Thanksgiving sanctifies everything. It brightens everything up with God's presence. Complaining and murmuring on the other hand sucks the life and joy out of everything. The supernaturally empowered believer makes his life a complaint-free zone.

Everything that we can thank God for becomes holy and blessed and radiant with the life of His kingdom. People often think that if something is religious it must be holy; and for something to be holy it must be religious. The most down to earth activity is holy if it is done with an attitude of thanksgiving towards God, and the most exalted religious activity is unholy if done in the wrong attitude.

It is not the religiosity of an activity but the attitude of thanksgiving towards God that makes it holy. The ordinary activities of daily life do not have to pull us away from God's kingdom but through thanksgiving they can become charged with the presence of God.

CHAPTER 2

THE HABIT OF PRAYER

Prayer is a unique gift from God to those who believe in Him. It is the most powerful force on the earth.

The power of prayer lies not in the prayer but in God who stands at the other end of our cry.

Prayer is the channel by which God's mercies are welcomed on the earth. It receives and welcomes heaven's help, heaven's life and heaven's rule on the earth and into our lives. Without it the earth would be "God forsaken". With it God's help and mercies are received.

"And without faith it is impossible to please him (God). For whoever would draw near to God must believe that he exists and that he rewards those who seek him." (Hebrews 11:6)

The most supernaturally empowered believers know how to approach God in prayer with confidence, and through it draw down God's resources and blessings on their own lives and the lives of others.

As we come to God through the atoning sacrifice of Jesus we can approach Him with great boldness.

"Therefore, brethren, since we have confidence to enter the sanctuary by the blood of Jesus, by the new and living way which he opened for us through the curtain, that is, through his flesh, and since we have a great priest over the house of God, let us draw near with a true heart in full assurance of faith, with our hearts sprinkled clean from an evil conscience and our bodies washed with pure water. Let us hold fast the confession of our hope without wavering, for he who promised is faithful." (Hebrews 10:19-23)

PRAYER IS WELCOMING GOD'S WILL

Through prayer we use our will to consciously, deliberately and confidently embrace God's will, mercies and blessings into our lives.

- Through it we embrace the plans, purposes and call of God on our lives.

- Through it we receive from God the inner strengthening and outer anointing to become open channels of the kingdom of God.

- Through prayer the presence, power, purposes and mercies of God come flooding into our lives and situations.

Prayer is not forcing our will on God or 'twisting His arm.' It is asking God to do what He has already revealed He wants to do. Prayer is related to God's will.

Since prayer is related to God's will, it is related to God's word, which is the revelation of God's will.

"And this is the confidence which we have in him, that if we ask anything according to his will he hears us. And if we know that he hears us in whatever we ask, we know that we have obtained the requests made of him." (I John 5:14-15) This is amazing! We can be sure our prayer will be answered if we ask according to His will. If we ask according to His will, we can consider it done!

When we read the Bible we discover what His will is. We are now in the position to pray with confidence, because we know that our prayers are in line with His will, and will, therefore, be answered.

WHY IS PRAYER NECESSARY?

When man was created he was given dominion upon the earth. We were given dominion over the earth to rule over it in partnership with God's resources and counsel. Prayer is necessary because God will not impose His will upon us. He will not bypass our free will. He reveals His will to us and then invites us to embrace and accept it. He waits until we come into agreement with Him. *"Truly, I say to you, whatever you bind on earth shall be bound in heaven, and whatever you loose on earth shall be loosed in heaven. Again I say to you, if two of you agree on earth touching anything it will be done for them by my Father in heaven."* (Matthew 18:18-19)

God waits for us to come into agreement with His will. We can bind ourselves to His will and loose ourselves from all that is not His will. We can release His will into our situations, and loose ourselves from that which is not His will. In this way His kingdom advances and replaces what is not His will with His will. The curse is replaced with the blessing and chaos with His benign order.

The principle of prayer is that earth moves heaven. Heaven waits for earth to come into agreement. What an awesome responsibility and privilege!

This is why God says: *"Thus says the LORD, the Holy One of Israel, and his Maker, Ask me of things to come concerning my sons, and concerning the work of my hands command you me."* (Isaiah 45:11)

"Therefore I tell you, whatever you ask in prayer, believe that you have received it, and it will be yours." (Mark 11:24)

"Whatever you ask in my name, I will do it, that the Father may be glorified in the Son." (John 14:13)

"You did not choose me, but I chose you and appointed you that you should go and bear fruit and that your fruit should abide; so that whatever you ask the Father in my name, he may give it to you." (John 15:16)

God has given these prayer promises to all believers so that His will can be done on earth as it is in heaven. The key of prayer is the most important key that Jesus left with

His followers. It is the greatest key of the supernaturally empowered believer.

Prayer is not the refuge of the helpless. It is the powerful equipment of those who embrace and release God's kingdom on the earth.

ASPECTS OF PRAYER

The believer's prayer, unlike the prayer of the pagan (or the one untutored in the scriptures), has power because it is based on:

- the revelation of God's will

- confident access to God through the blood of Jesus

- the engagement of our will and lives to receive and seek His will

- the use of our tongue to make our requests known and to speak forth the will of God into our situations, and

- the authority of the name of Jesus

The prayer of the supernaturally empowered believer is a co-operative enterprise between him and God to bring God's will to bear in the situations of need.

The prayer of the pagan, or the one unlettered in the Word of God is based on hope, wish and guess. The prayer of the believer, on the other hand, is based on the knowledge of God's will i.e. the knowledge of what God wants to do. It is based on a revelation of what God's will is. We know that God wants to improve things on the earth. His will is better than the status quo. Prayer is grounded on the knowledge that

God's will, when it is released into any situation, will bring changes for the better. These changes may be changes in us, changes in the attitudes of others, changes in our perception, or some other change in the situation itself.

PRAY & SAY

The believer's prayer is a compassionate partnership to establish God's benign will on the earth and to replace oppression with blessing. Prayer is not simply a matter of projecting thoughts into the air. It is not a mere devotional exercise. It is serious divine business. It is the act of transacting spiritual business with God Himself with our words. In law we transact business contracts with our written signatures. In the spirit we transact spiritual business with our spoken words.

Jesus warned us not to pray as the pagans, who pray without authority and without assurance. He empowers us to pray with authority from the relationship with God the Father that He has established for us and to pray using the authority of His name.

When you pray say: *"Our Father in heaven hallowed be thy name thy kingdom come thy will be done on earth as it is in heaven...."* (Matthew 6:9)

Since prayer is based on the revealed will of God we can take the promises of God as revealed in His word and ask Him to fulfill them in our lives. We can then declare them over our lives.

Most believers are untrained in the use of their tongue. They do not realize its importance in advancing God's will in their lives. *"You shall also decree a thing, and it shall be established for you: and the light shall shine upon your ways."* (Job 22:28)

"Truly I say to you, whoever says to this mountain 'Be taken up and cast into the sea,' and does not doubt in heart but believes that what he says will come to pass, it will be done for him". (Mark 11:23)

Supernaturally empowered believers know the importance of using their tongues to release God's will into situations. Through it God's will is embraced, received and advanced in the situations of their lives.

PRAYER & DECLARATION IN THE NAME OF JESUS

"And whatsoever ye shall ask in my name, that will I do, that the Father may be glorified in the Son. If ye shall ask anything in my name, that will I do." (John 14:13-14)

"You have not chosen Me, but I have chosen you and ordained you that you should go and bring forth fruit, and that your fruit should remain; that whatever you shall ask of the Father in my name, He may give it to you." (Jn. 15:16)

"And in that day you shall ask Me nothing. Truly, truly, I say to you, whatever you shall ask the Father in My name, He will give you." (John 16:23)

42

This is an invitation to approach God the Father and to use Jesus' name to invoke God's will into situations. We approach God not on the grounds of our own piety but through the blood of Jesus and using His name we pray with His authority for God's will to come forth on the earth.

> Prayer is not the refuge of the helpless. It is the powerful equipment of those who embrace and release God's kingdom on the earth.

We can have tremendous boldness and authority in prayer because Jesus has given us His name. By giving us His name we can act as His delegated authority. As His delegated authority we can invoke the will of His Father to move God's will and plan from heaven into earth. We can also, in His name, decree His will into situations over which He has given us authority.

"Before now you have asked nothing in my name; ask and you shall receive, that your joy may be full." (John 16:24)

Jesus gives us His name to use in vertical prayer upward to God the Father. We can also use His name to command God's will into situations. This prayer is not to God but a command from God through us as His delegated authority.

The prayer of command is used in ministry – speaking God's will into situations and commanding oppressive spirits from situations. Every believer should be trained to use the name of Jesus in this way. We are not imposing our will on situations but we are imposing God's will into situations.

WARFARE & PRAYER

Prayer advances God's will against that which is not His will. Joshua knew that God had given the Land of Promise to the children of Israel. He also knew that he had to fight to possess God's promises. God's promises are not automatically fulfilled in our lives. We must embrace them in prayer and faith and advance them by declarative faith. The believer's fight is not physical but it is spiritual. We are aware that there are oppressive spirits that resist the advance of God's kingdom and prevent His will being done. In prayer we ask that God's will overcome and replace the darkness. We also use the name of Jesus to take authority over spirits working on the earth, which resist the advance of God's will. In this way we can impose the will of God against the will of the evil one.

PRAYER IN THREE DIMENSIONS

God is looking for people to stand in the gap

in prayer to link God's mercy with man's need.

"And I sought for a man among them who should build up the wall and stand in the breach before me for the land, that I should not destroy it; but I found none." (Eze. 22: 30)

Prayer operates in three dimensions:

- upward to God the Father in Jesus' name
- outward declaring the will of God into our lives and situations, in Jesus' name
- downward, in Jesus' name against the spirits that hinder the will of God being done

Supernaturally empowered believers know how to operate in all three dimensions of prayer. They pray vertically, horizontally and downwardly. The effective prayer of the believer requires skillfulness in all three dimensions.

Our authority is based on the access we have to God as new creations and redeemed people through the blood of Jesus. Many believers miss their authority in prayer because they look at their feelings or sense of worthiness. Our authority is not in our perfection but in the name of Jesus and our desire to see His will advance in the situations we pray for.

Jesus has actually delegated to those in union and submission to Him the privilege of using His name, and acting in His name.

"Before now you have asked nothing in My name; ask and you shall receive, that your joy may be full. I have spoken these things to you in parables, but the time is coming when I shall no more speak to you in parables, but I will show you plainly of the Father. At that day you will ask in My name; and I do not say to you that I will pray to the Father for you, for the Father Himself loves you, because you have loved Me and have believed that I came out from God." (John 16:24-27)

When we accept the benefits of the Atonement we receive the Holy Spirit, adoption into God's family, redemption from the curse and the right to use His name. This gives the believer in Jesus a far higher level of authority in prayer than any other kind of worshipper. It is the restoration of what was lost in Adam, and it is the supernatural equipment of the supernaturally empowered believer.

HINDRANCES TO PRAYER

The greatest hindrance to prayer is unforgiveness. Jesus said that we cannot even begin to pray if we have unforgiveness towards others. *"And whenever you stand praying, forgive, if you have anything against any one; so that your Father also who is in heaven may forgive you your trespasses."* (Mark 11:25)

Unforgiveness breaks the circuit of communication with God. Therefore before we pray we must remove any unforgiveness against ourselves, others or God. For the same reason the prayer of a husband who is harsh towards his wife will be hindered. *"Likewise you husbands, live considerately with your wives, bestowing honor on the woman as the weaker sex, since you are joint heirs of the grace of life, in order that your prayers may not be hindered."* (1 Peter 3:7)

Prayer is also hindered if we try to appropriate the promises of His kingdom without really believing in Him or surrendering our lives to Him. *"Seek first the kingdom of God and his righteousness and all these things will be added unto you."* (Matthew 6:33) We cannot ask the Lord for "all things" unless we are seeking His kingdom.

To have the benefits of His kingdom without surrendering to His kingdom is impossible. It is like trying to have the benefit of the sunshine while remaining indoors. Jesus said: *"If you abide in Me, and My words abide in you, you shall ask what you will, and it shall be done to you."* (John 15:7) Remaining in union with Jesus' life and words is

47

the key to fruitfulness and answered prayer. Our prayers are hindered when we move away from His way of perfect love towards all.

> 'With words we govern men.'
> – Benjamin Disraeli

PRAYER - AN ONGOING LIFE HABIT

The greatest prayers are not "give me" prayers but "make me" prayers. The supernatural believer develops a lifestyle of continual communication with God. It never ceases. We constantly ask for God's will to be done in our lives. We constantly ask that more and more of His promises be fulfilled in our lives and for Him to transform us to the image of His Son.

Prayer has seven major spheres:
1. for ourselves
2. for our families
3. for our local church
4. for our cities
5. for our nations
6. for Israel, and
7. for the harvest fields

WORSHIPPERS

The supernaturally empowered believer has perfect access to God's presence through the blood of Jesus. In addition, the Spirit has come to live in Him and from deep within cries out "Abba, Father." The Holy Spirit cries out for intimate communication with God. *"And because you are sons, God has sent forth the Spirit of His Son into your hearts, crying, Abba, Father."* (Galatians 4:6)

Prayer is a not only a matter of receiving and releasing God's will, it is also a loving communion with God. There is an "Abba, Father" cry in the heart of every supernaturally empowered believer that longs for communication with Him. We call this kind of communication with God "worship". Love is maintained by communication and as we communicate with Him in worship, thanksgiving, awareness of His presence and listening, our love relationship with Him grows.

Worship is not just something we do in a group setting with musical instruments and singing. Singing may be used in worship but it is not the essential part of worship. Worship is pouring out our heart in thanksgiving and acknowledgment to our God and to our Savior. It is not a matter of ritual - it is a matter of the heart.

> The greatest prayers are not "give me" prayers but "make me" prayers.

Jesus quotes God's complaint with ritualistic and formal worship: *"This people draws near to Me with their mouth, and honors Me with their lips, but their heart is far from Me."* (Mt. 15:8)

The point is that we may go through the motions of worship without putting our hearts in it. God is looking for people who really love, really honor and really appreciate Him, not because they have to, but because they love to. This is God's greatest desire: people who will respond to His love with all their hearts, and enter a living partnership with Him.

One of the tragedies of Christianity is that, for everyone who does worship the Lord from the heart, there are many more who simply go through religious motions of worshipping Him. If we are true worshippers 'in spirit and in truth' we will walk in His ways and obey His commands.

This is about to change as the Spirit of God deals with institutions that promote this kind of insincerity. He is raising up a new generation of supernaturally empowered believers of every age whose number one goal in life is to please Him, honor Him, obey Him and pour out their lives before Him as a sacrifice of thanksgiving.

"But the hour is coming, and now is, when the true worshippers shall worship the Father in spirit and in truth; for the Father seeks such to worship Him. God is a spirit, and they who worship Him must worship in spirit and in truth." (John 4:23-24)

As we become worshippers, our relationship with God - Father, Son and Holy Spirit - becomes the most important relationship in our lives. When God occupies a greater part of our thoughts we become more and more aware of His presence with us. Such believers live their lives to an audience of ONE. They live to please Him rather than to impress people. *"I have set the LORD always before me: because he is at my right hand, I shall not be moved."* (Ps. 16:8) The most supernaturally empowered believers keep the Lord before them continually. They cultivate a sense of His presence, and become more and more aware that He is with them always.

"Cast all your cares on the Lord because He cares for you." (1 Peter 5:7) God invites us to throw our problems at His feet. If something concerns us it concerns God also ... nothing is too small or too big for Him who created the universe and yet knows every hair of our head. The

effectiveness of the believer is entirely based on prayer, which links our lives with the help and intervening presence of God Himself. We have many responsibilities in life but we are not expected to fulfill them without God's resources and abundant help, which come to us when we ask.

CHAPTER 3

THE HABIT OF RECEIVING

"His divine power has given to us all things that pertain to life and godliness, through the knowledge of Him who has called us to glory and virtue." (2 Peter 1:3)

"For who makes you to differ? And what have you that you didst not receive? But if you did receive it, why do you glory as if you had not received it?" (1 Cor. 4:7)

"And out of His fullness we all have received, and grace for grace." (John 1:16)

"But my God shall supply all your need according to His riches in glory by Christ Jesus." (Phil. 4:19)

Everything we have and are we have received either directly or indirectly from God. If we have gifts, abilities, intelligence, anointing, health or any other blessing it is only because we received it.

RECEIVING THROUGH THE CHANNEL OF FAITH

Many of God's blessings come to us simply through the natural process as a gift packet with our creation. Such gifts are passively received. However, a great many of His spiritual blessings, though offered freely, have to be actively received by faith.

To receive by faith is to receive from God through the process of acknowledging one's need and asking. We can only receive from God what we know He wants to give us in the first place. We, therefore, need the scriptures to know what we can freely receive from God, because they reveal what God wants to give us. In this sense the scriptures are rather like a catalog, which lets us know what a retailer has available for ordering!

God does not force His spiritual gifts and blessings on us because He respects our free will. However, He reveals through the Bible what He wants to give us so that we can freely receive them.

The most effective believers are effective receivers because they constantly welcome, embrace, hunger and yearn for all God has to offer them. They want:

- to be all that God wants them to be

- to do all that He wants them to do,

- and to have all that He wants them to have.

To "receive" means "to welcome, accept and take". God's blessings are not automatic. They must be actively received and humbly taken from Him. There is a cliché (not from the Bible but from Aesop's Fables) that says: "God helps those who help themselves." The truth is that God cannot help those who refuse His help.

The supernaturally empowered believer lives in a continuous flow of blessing and provision that flows to him moment by moment from God. We are swimming in a sea of His blessing and provision. No matter how many difficulties and problems we face we have access to an infinite supply of resources and provision from God. *"But my God shall supply all your need according to His riches in glory by Christ Jesus."* (Phil. 4:19) This is the condition of every believer.

As we continue on with Jesus and keep His word before us we maintain our vital connection with God. In this relationship we continually draw from His life and receive from His goodness and generosity one blessing after another. *"And from His fullness we have all received one blessing after another."* (John 1:16 LB)

RECEIVE WHAT?

The New Testament is a treasure trove revealing what God has made available to us through the work of Jesus.

This is why it is called "a testament." A testament is a written declaration of what is bequeathed to a beneficiary at the death of the Testator.

The New Testament reveals what Jesus has bequeathed to those who come to Him and follow Him.

"Blessed be the God and Father of our Lord Jesus Christ, who has blessed us in Christ with every spiritual blessing in the heavenly places." (Ephesians 1:3)

These benefits of redemption are made available by the saving work of Jesus and are to be received with faith and thanksgiving.

> The most supernaturally empowered believers are effective receivers. They constantly welcome, embrace, hunger, and yearn for all that God has for them.

"Bless the LORD, O my soul, and forget not all his benefits." (Psalm 103:2) The thought here is that if we don't actively remember and appropriate these benefits, they lie like unopened gifts.

These benefits include the following:

- Forgiveness (2 Cor. 5:17-21)

- Salvation (Ephesians 2:8)

- Redemption (Gal. 3:13; Eph.1:7)

- Adoption (Romans 8:15)

- Sonship (Romans 8:15)

- Authority (Luke 9:1)

- The Holy Spirit (John 20:22)

- Spiritual power (Acts 1:8)

- The fruit of the Spirit (Gal. 5:22)

- The gifts of the Spirit (1 Cor. 14:1)

- The Word of God (James 1:21)

- Healing (Luke 6:18; Acts 8:7; 28:9)

- Instruction in good works (2 Tim. 3:16)

- Promises to live by (Hebrews 11:33)

- Guidance & direction (James 1:5)

- Every spiritual blessing (Eph.1:3)

- Practical provision (Phil. 4:19)

- The blessings of Abraham (Gal. 3:14; Gen. 24:1)

- Ministry (John 20:21)

- God's maintaining mercies on our spirit soul and body (1 Thess. 5:23)

- ETC. ETC. ETC. ETC. ETC.

We maintain God's benefits in our lives by continuing to receive them through an attitude of receptivity and continual thankfulness.

Jesus tells us to receive our provision from God on a day-by-day basis. "Give us this day our daily bread' is the daily request to God for all we need, by those who know that they are completely dependent on Him for everything.

Many, growing accustomed to God's goodness, become presumptuous and develop the attitude: "I have received this and that from God and now I am complete." They neglect to ask and to acknowledge the source of every blessing. They take everything for granted and attribute their blessings and successes to their own cleverness or to mere natural law. They become presumptuous.

Presumption is the opposite of receiving - it is taking things for granted. It is the failure to receive and appropriate that which God is giving. By receiving consciously we reverse presumption and continue the flow of receptivity from God. He wants us to receive from Him on a daily basis all the spiritual, mental, physical and material benefits we need to conduct our lives on the earth. In addition, He has new mercies to give us each day: *"The steadfast love of the LORD never ceases, his mercies never come to an end; they are new every morning; great is thy faithfulness."* (Lam. 3:22-23) He who created the galaxies has fresh things for us each day. As we continue to receive His new mercies, life with Him is never boring. It becomes an adventure in discovery of the dimensions of His love.

DON'T FORGET TO ASK

God's benefits do not come automatically. We must use our wills and ask. Some are too proud to ask. Jesus tells us to ask. *"Ask and it will be given to you, seek and you will find, knock and the door will be opened."* (Mt. 7:7) We are to ask the Father in His name and so become good receivers.

James says: *"You have not because you ask not."* (James 4:2) Supernaturally empowered believers learn to embrace, accept and receive all that God has made available to them.

Today much of the church is in spiritual poverty because we have not asked and have not received our full inheritance. Others have become spiritually poor through presumption. They are relying on past experiences of blessings to sustain

59

them and fail to receive fresh infillings of God's life, love and Spirit.

OUR AMAZING INHERITANCE

Have you ever been tempted to envy those who have inherited vast wealth from their family? Perhaps your grandfather or father was not able to leave you an inheritance. But God has left an amazing inheritance to every human being. The great tragedy is that the majority of people on the planet have no idea of this inheritance. They are like paupers, starving in a tenement slum that are heirs to a vast inheritance they know nothing about.

"But how are men to call upon him in whom they have not believed?

And how are they to believe in him of whom they have never heard? And how are they to hear without a preacher?" (Romans 10:14)

For someone to become an heir, four things must happen:

1. they must be left something in a will or testament

2. the person who made the will must die

3. they must learn about their inheritance, and

4. they must receive their inheritance.

The New Testament is called a "testament" because it represents the last will and testament of Jesus. He died to bring us into an inheritance with God. Our sin had blocked us from this inheritance but His atonement restores us to our inheritance. The heritage that Adam lost, Jesus restores and more.

"Therefore he (Jesus) is the mediator of a new covenant, so that those who are called may receive the promised eternal inheritance, since a death has occurred which redeems them from the transgressions under the first covenant. For where a will is involved, the death of the one who made it must be established. For a will takes effect only at death, since it is not in force as long as the one who made it is alive." (Hebrews 9:15-17)

Jesus' death not only atones for our sins, and cancels the curse, but it also brings us into an amazing inheritance. It will take us all eternity to discover the full treasures that are involved in this inheritance. However, we can begin the journey of discovery now.

"The Spirit himself bearing witness with our spirit that we are children of God, and if children, then heirs, heirs of God and fellow heirs with Christ, provided we suffer with him in order that we may also be glorified with him". (Romans 8:16-17)

As Peter puts it, we have been *"born again and to an inheritance which is imperishable undefiled, and unfading, kept in heaven for you."* (1 Peter 1:4)

The Bible says that we are blessed with the blessings of Abraham through the death of Jesus.

"Christ redeemed us from the curse of the law, having become a curse for us. For it is written, 'Cursed be every one who hangs on a tree'- that in Christ Jesus the blessing of Abraham might come upon the Gentiles, that we might receive the promise of the Spirit through faith." (Galatians 3:13)

But what are the blessings of Abraham? Genesis 24:1 tells us that Abraham was blessed 'in all things'. So the blessings of Abraham are to be blessed in all things! That's comprehensive! He was blessed in his relationship with God in his health, in his finances and with the blessing of being a blessing to others.

Now, because of the atoning work of Jesus, through faith the blessings that came on Abraham can come on every believer.

If this were not enough for us Paul also tells us that we have been blessed *"with every spiritual blessing."* (Ephesians 1:3) In addition to the blessings of Abraham, God wants to bless us with every spiritual blessing. These are first, fellowship and friendship with God, then revelation and

---

experience of His love, the fruit of the Spirit, wisdom, love, anointing, fellowship with God, humility, prayerfulness, godliness, favor, fruitfulness and more.

It is the responsibility of the heir to search out his inheritance and then to claim it and walk in it. We cannot claim what is not ours, nor inherit what has not been bequeathed, but we can inherit all that God has left for us.

The student of the bible searches out his inheritance and progressively enters the fullness of it. This requires study, discovery, obedience and constant asking and receiving.

RECEIVE THROUGH OTHER PEOPLE

All of us owe our existence and life not only to God but also to other people. We are held in existence by a vast network of people. We often take these people for granted but we owe so much to them. We owe our quality of life to a huge range of people - from food growers, truck drivers, shopkeepers, politicians, government officials, electricians, health care givers, educators, mechanics, plumbers, electricians, builders, road workers - without whom our lives could not function. Above all, we owe our existence to our parents to whom we owe special honor.

We receive endless help from an almost infinite chain of other people. The best believers recognize that God's help comes not only directly but also through this great network of other people who help, encourage, educate, and serve us.

Life in the kingdom of God is a vast web of people being helped by God, and giving and receiving help. Some, through an exaggerated sense of independence, find it difficult to receive from others. Peter had this problem when Jesus went to wash his feet.

He was embarrassed to receive such menial service from the King of the Universe.

Ruth changed history by accepting help from Boaz. Jesus, our greatest example, allowed the Samaritan woman to give Him something before He brought a blessing to her, and He was sustained and helped by many others.

"And it came to pass soon afterwards, that he went about through cities and villages, preaching and bringing the good tidings of the kingdom of God, and with him the twelve, and certain women who had been healed of evil spirits and infirmities: Mary that was called Magdalene, from whom seven demons had gone out, and Joanna the wife of Chua, Herod's steward, and Susanna, and many others,

who ministered unto Him of their substance." (Luke 8:1-3)

It is humbling to have to receive help from God and other people but it is absolutely essential. Supernaturally empowered believers never manipulate people but are always open to receive help from others and to allow God to use people to help them.

Every believer lives in a constant river of blessing, which God brings to us directly and through other people. Acknowledging this and receiving them makes us interdependent and creates a network of loving relationships.

CHAPTER 4

THE HABIT OF GIVING

Giving is not primarily a duty - it is a privilege. It is the expression of a heart that loves. Endless appeals for money constantly remind us of our duty to give. This is unfortunate because it makes it difficult to separate the privilege of giving from the pressure of appeals.

Philanthropic giving harnesses universal laws of generosity. Giving blesses not only the receiver but it blesses the giver even more. As Jesus said, *"There is a greater blessing in giving than in receiving."* (Acts 20:35) Giving not only aligns us with universal laws of the universe, it also increases our alignment with God's promises and supply. God observes the giving of the believer and rewards it. *"Your Father who sees in secret will reward you."* (Matthew 6:4)

"He who supplies seed to the sower and bread for food will supply and multiply your resources

and increase the harvest of your righteousness." (2 Cor. 9:10)

God actively involves Himself in the finances of generous givers.

GIVING & ABRAHAM'S BLESSINGS

Abraham was uniquely chosen by God to be blessed. God promised to bless him and to make him a blessing to all nations.

God gives to us so that not only are our own needs met, but that we also may meet the needs of others.

God's plan was to bless this man and to extend through his offspring the same blessing to all nations. *"I will bless you and make you a blessing and in you all the families of the earth shall be blessed."* (Genesis 12:3)

The conditions for the extension of these blessings were realized when Jesus died for the sins of the world. The curse of sin and guilt, which is common to all men, was borne and broken by Jesus. Since Jesus has borne the curse of our sins, Abraham's blessings can come on all sincere believers through faith. *"Christ redeemed us from the curse of the law, having become a curse for us; for it is written, Cursed is every one that hangs on a tree: that upon the Gentiles might come the blessing of Abraham in Christ Jesus; that we might receive the promise of the Spirit through faith."* (Galatians 3:13-14)

We are told that Abraham was blessed in all things: *"Now Abraham was old, well advanced in years; and the LORD had blessed Abraham in all things."* (Genesis 24:1) God blesses *us* in all things too as He did Abraham when we believe, receive and obey. In addition He empowers us to be a blessing to others. Having received blessings we can become a blessing to others. The curse has been borne and we can now be a blessing. This is our destiny. We are blessed to be a blessing.

God not only blesses us for our own sake but also equips us with the resources to bless others. He gives to us so that, not only are our own needs met, but we also may meet the needs of others. Giving is a major part of the practical expression of Jesus' new commandment: *"Love one another as I have loved you."* (John 13:34)

GIVE WHAT?

When we think of giving we usually think of giving financially. It includes financial generosity, but it is much more.

The relationship between the believer and Jesus is like a marriage relationship. As we enter into covenant relationship with God, God's resources are made available to us and ours are made available to Him. Guess who gets the best of the bargain! Our sharing with God, however, is not a bargain but a mutual sharing based on the covenant with God in the blood of Jesus that has merged our lives with His.

The believer's giving flows from the reality of his covenant relationship with God. God makes His infinite supply available to us as we need it, and we make our meager resources available to Him also. The resources of God belong to those who belong to Him. As the father said to the elder brother: *"Son, you are always with me and all I have is yours."* (Luke 15:31)

The primary giving of the believer is, therefore, not financial - it is the giving of himself to God in the same way as a husband gives himself to his wife, and a wife *gives herself to her husband.*

"We want you to know, brethren, about the grace of God which has been shown in the churches of Macedonia, for in a severe test of affliction, their abundance of joy and their extreme poverty have overflowed in a wealth of liberality on their part.

For they gave according to their means, as I can testify, and beyond their means, of their own free will ... but first they gave themselves to the Lord and to us by the will of God." (2 Cor. 8:1-5)

"It is possible to give without loving,
but it is impossible to love without giving."
– Richard Braunstein

These believers became very generous because they had first given themselves to God. They were free to be generous not because they were rich but because they were sure of the reality of God's faithfulness to them.

God first looks for us to give ourselves to Him. He invites us to come into a loving, sharing union with Him that can only be compared to a loving marriage. He wants us loosed from the world and available to Him. The kingdom of God is the loving wedding of our hearts with God's heart, our plans with His plans, and our lives with His life.

"Present your bodies a living sacrifice which is your reasonable service." (Romans 12:1)

Once we make ourselves available for the interests of God and His kingdom then every other kind of giving comes into right perspective.

If we give our money without giving our hearts it means little. Giving our money is simply the overflow and fruit of our loving union with Him.

Giving is not something measurable by a calculator. It operates in a spiritual dimension of the heart. It is the response of the heart to the boundless loving of God who gave His Son for us and gives us all things in Him.

GIVING IS GREATER THAN RECEIVING

"Give, and it will be given to you; good measure, pressed down, shaken together, running over, will be put into your lap. For the measure you give will be the measure you get back." (Luke 6:38)

It is every man's destiny to be our brother's keeper. Giving makes us a channel of help and blessing to others. It is one of the practical ways we express love for others and fulfill the great command to "love our neighbor as ourselves."

Giving relates us to the world and the people around us, as we ought to. We were made to be blessed and to be a blessing. We were made to be receivers and to be givers.

To give out of compulsion or from mere religious duty has no reward or blessing, but giving out of a heart of compassion and love brings joy and life to the giver and to the receiver. *"If I give away all I have, and if I deliver my body to be burned, but have not love, I gain nothing."* (1 Corinthians 13:3)

Though no one can give what he has not received, Jesus says, *"It is more blessed to give than to receive."* (Acts 20:35)

Being a blessing to others through serving and giving promotes us to greater levels of blessing.

Giving to others, as love directs, actually enlarges our capacity to receive more and give more. The essence of the kingdom of God and the message of Jesus is that we enter the highest joy when we all become receivers and transmitters of blessings.

Receiving with thanksgiving enriches and enlarges us, but giving with joy enlarges us even more. Receiving brings blessing to our lives, but giving brings an even greater blessing. "The point is this: he who sows sparingly will also reap sparingly, and he who sows bountifully will also reap bountifully. And God is able to provide you with every blessing in abundance, so that you may always have enough of everything and may provide in abundance for every good work.

As it is written, *"He scatters abroad, he gives to the poor; his righteousness endures for ever."* *He who supplies seed to the sower and bread for food will supply and multiply your resources and increase the harvest of your righteousness".* (2 Cor. 9:6-9)

GIVE TO WHOM?

Scripture teaches another kind of giving that is only available to the believer – giving to God. This kind of giving expresses our love for God and our recognition that He is the source of all blessing.

God is the Possessor of everything so He Himself does not need our gift. However, the only finances available to Him to use on the earth are those, which have been released to His use (He is not a counterfeiter). Through the giving of the believers the work of the Lord can advance. When giving is withheld God's work is hindered.

In the days of the Temple believers were required to bring the tithe (one tenth of their income) to the Lord for the work of the Temple and for the provision of the Levites.

Today God's work is not located in a physical temple. What we have now is a body of people who are indwelt by the Spirit of God. This is the temple of the Body of Christ of which every believer is a part. Since the "once for all" sacrifice of Jesus it is no longer necessary to offer sacrifice for sins. What is necessary now is to proclaim the fact and the benefits of the great "once for all" sacrifice. When the benefits of this sacrifice are proclaimed everywhere, God's mercy and blessing can be known and received *"to the ends of the earth."*

Our giving to spiritual causes no longer goes to a physical temple but it goes to advance the work of the Lord in our local area and the work of God's kingdom around the world. The body of Christ is a temple bringing the benefits of God's mercy to the ends of the earth. When we bring our money to the temple today we make it available for the manifold work of the Body of Christ.

Our special obligation is to give to our local church (Ephesians 4:16), to those who instruct us in the word, to missioners (Galatians 6:6), to the poor and to the widow and orphan (Matthew 25; James 1:27).

Since God has promised to bless those who bless the children of Abraham Isaac and Jacob (Genesis 12:3) it is good to bless the Jewish people financially and in other ways. God continues to work with them to fulfill their special place in His sovereign plan to return them to the Land of Promise. We seek to bless what God is blessing, to help what God is helping, and to love that which He loves.

GIVE HOW MUCH?

For the believer the question is not "How much must I give?" but "how much can I give?"

The scriptures warn us not to give under compulsion or under impulse, but to give out of love and in a spirit of cheerful hilarity.

Since the New Testament believer's giving is an act of freedom and not compulsion, he can deliberately decide and budget how much to give. There is no doubt that the generous spirit of the New Testament indicates at least a tenth of our gross income. We who are blessed by God should immediately become blessers of others and supporters of the Lord's work through our finances. God calls withholding the tithe and offerings "robbery." When we withhold our tithe and offerings we rob the Body of Christ of the money it needs to do its work.

"Will man rob God? Yet you are robbing me. But you say, 'How are we robbing thee?' In your tithes and offerings. You are cursed with a curse, for you are robbing me; the whole nation of you. Bring the full tithes into the storehouse, that there may be food in my house; and thereby put me to the test, says the LORD of hosts, if I will not open the windows of heaven for you and pour down for you

an overflowing blessing. I will rebuke the devourer for you, so that it will not destroy the fruits of your soil; and your vine in the field shall not fail to bear, says the LORD of hosts." (Malachi 3:8-11)

In Biblical days the tithe was from the produce of the work. The farmer gave a tithe of his crop and the hired man a tithe of his income, before other expenses. The farmer was not required to give a tithe of his farm or a tithe of his trees but a tithe of the production of his farm. So too God does not normally require us to give a tithe of our estate each year but tithes and offerings off the production of the estate. In this way our work becomes a partnership with God and a vital part of His ministry on the earth. Work and business become sanctified and sacred and the divide between sacred and secular is removed.

As basic training for giving, the Bible teaches tithing. Paul says *"the Law was our schoolteacher until Christ came."* (Galatians 3:24) The law taught tithing. Jesus says our righteousness should exceed that of the scribes and the Pharisees i.e. go deeper and further than the giving of the scribes and Pharisees who tithed. *"For I tell you, unless your righteousness exceeds that of the scribes and Pharisees, you will never enter the kingdom of heaven."* (Matthew 5:20)

"But woe to you Pharisees! For you tithe mint and rue and every herb, and neglect justice and the love of God; these you ought to have done, without neglecting the others." (Luke 11:42)

Here Jesus said that they were right to tithe, but tithing and religious observance are no substitutes for love. You can give without love but you cannot love without giving. We can safely say New Testament believers should seek to give at least a tithe of their gross income and increase this as the Lord blesses and prospers them. Even the poorest believer can tithe. As he does so, he is declaring by his action that he believes the yoke of poverty is broken over his life and he is now beginning to be a blessing to others.

In the New Testament, because *"Christ has redeemed us from the curse of the law having become a curse for us"* (Galatians 3:13) there is no curse for not tithing, but there is a blessing for giving. Believers should not be threatened to give but encouraged to give as an expression of love and as a blessing.

GIVE FREELY & GIVE LOVINGLY

When Abraham tithed to Melchizedek, the giver (Abraham) controlled where His tithe went.

Later, In the Temple days the receivers (the Levites) controlled where the tithe went.

Since Jesus' day we are no longer under the religious ordinances of the Temple priesthood. There is a new priest, Jesus and His priesthood is not Levitical but *"after the order of Melchizedek."* (Hebrews 7:11)

And so our giving today in the New Testament order should be patterned from the model of Abraham and Melchizedek. This means that the giver should decide where to put his tithe. The receiver should not demand the tithe but receive them. The receiver does not exercise control or ownership over the giver. The giver is related to God and God directs his giving.

Melchizedek demanded nothing from Abraham but received from him. Believers today should not be hounded by legalistic controlling demands for their money but should learn to give generously, responsibly and freely. As Jesus says, *"freely you have received, freely give."* (Matthew 10:8) They should be encouraged to give and then respond in love to give to the Lord and His work as they freely decide and as the Spirit directs.

Those who serve the Lord should learn to look to God to send people to help them. It is a healthy thing to lean on God who uses people to meet our needs but it is manipulative to obligate people to meet them. In the best giving - receiving relationships the giver does not seek to control the receiver and the receiver does not pressurize or manipulate the giver.

The most effective giving is done in a spirit of love, freedom and faith. That which is done by mere obligation without love does not profit us (1 Corinthians 13:3). Our generosity should flow from the love that the Holy Spirit generates in our hearts.

Giving in a spirit of joy, love for God, where there is no coercion, fear, or manipulation is one of the highest privileges of the believer.

"Each one must do as he has made up his mind, not reluctantly or under compulsion, for God loves a cheerful giver." (2 Cor. 9:7)

"I preferred to do nothing without your consent in order that your goodness might not be by compulsion but of your own free will." (Philemon 1:14)

The love of God and the Spirit of God will direct us to give. When we fail to give we not only deprive those who could be blessed by our generosity but we actually deprive ourselves of the enlargement of our heart and the increase God promises to those who are generous.

All supernaturally empowered believers are great givers. Let us ask God to give us generous hearts and enlarge our capacity to give and to bless. For the supernaturally empowered believer, giving is not a mere obligation - it is a lifestyle of fulfillment and expansion.

It is a thrill and a blessing. The most supernaturally empowered believers live to give.

"The generous soul will be enriched and he who waters will himself be watered" (Prov. 11:25)

"Now as you excel in everything - in faith, in utterance, in knowledge, in all earnestness, and in your love for us see that you excel in this gracious work (giving) also." (2 Cor. 8:7)

As we give we are aligning ourselves with God's love and mercy. We become partners with God in supplying the needs of His children. God entrusts us with finances to give to others and makes us channels of His ministry to help others. When our motives are not tied into personal wealth but to meet the needs of others there is almost no limit to what God can channel through us.

CHAPTER 5

THE HABIT OF FORGIVING

The habit of forgiveness is the most liberating habit of the effective disciple. The supernaturally empowered believer is energized with a new ability to forgive everyone because he carries the life of the Great Forgiver within Himself. All kingdom living is based on the primary reality that, through the atoning sacrifice of Jesus, our sins and lawless deeds are forgiven. Through faith in this great historical fact we stand in a new acquitted relationship with God.

"Come now, let us reason together, says the LORD: though your sins are like scarlet, they shall be as white as snow; though they are red like crimson, they shall become like wool." (Isaiah 1:18)

Jesus' death totally atoned for all our sins, mistakes, and wrong thinking. When we deliberately and personally appropriate these benefits our sins are forgiven, erased from the record, and we receive the gift of eternal life. God has no more charges against us because He has *"laid on Jesus the iniquity of all of us."* (Isaiah 53:6) Our part is to believe and receive this shockingly wonderful reality. God paid the penalty of our guilt while we were sinners.

"For while we were yet weak, in due season Christ died for the ungodly. For scarcely for a righteous man will one die: for peradventure for the good man some one would even dare to die. But God commends his own love toward us, in that, while we were yet sinners, Christ died for us. Much more then, being now justified by his blood, shall we be saved from the wrath of God through him." (Romans 5:6-9)

Forgiveness is not just that God overlooks our sin and says: "It doesn't matter'. He did not simply overlook our sin and forgive it - He paid a horrible price to bear our sin.

"All we like sheep had gone astray had turned every one to his own way, but the Lord has laid on Him the iniquity of us all." (Isaiah 53:6) The forgiveness available through the atoning sacrifice of Jesus is far greater than simply overlooking offence. God did not simply overlook our offences - He paid for them. The demands of justice were perfectly satisfied when Jesus took the wages of our sin.

The atoning sacrifice creates a new reality. The veil of the Temple is torn down. The barrier which sin created between man and God is breached. There is now an open heaven available to all who come through Jesus. With sins forgiven and cleansed we can now approach God without any sense of inferiority and guilt and stand - in spite of our past sins – in an acquitted relationship with Him. The love of God now comes pouring into our hearts by the Holy Spirit like water through an open tap.

"And you, being dead in your sins and the uncircumcision of your flesh, He has made alive together with Him, having forgiven you all trespasses, blotting out the handwriting of ordinances that was against us, which was contrary to us, and has taken it out of the way, nailing it to the cross." (Colossians 2:13-14)

Jesus has not destroyed the law but He has blotted out the written judgments against us. They have been nailed with Jesus to His cross and our guilt has been taken away!

"Therefore, since we are justified by faith, we have peace with God through our Lord Jesus Christ. Through him we have obtained access to this grace in which we stand, and we rejoice in our hope of sharing the glory of God. More than that, we rejoice in our sufferings, knowing that suffering produces endurance, and endurance produces character, and character produces hope, and hope

does not disappoint us, because God's love has been poured into our hearts through the Holy Spirit which has been given to us." (Rom. 5:1-5)

It is on the basis of this extraordinary emancipation from the real guilt of our sins that believers are empowered to be the best forgivers. To illustrate this, Jesus told a story (Matthew 18:23-25). A man who had amassed an enormous debt to his employer, and being totally unable to pay back the debt, threw himself at the employer's mercy. The employer then magnanimously forgave the debt and the man went away delighted. Released from his debt he was free to begin life anew.

Later another man incurred a minor debt to this forgiven worker. However, though he himself had received enormous mercy, he refused to show the same kind of mercy to his debtor. (It was like someone who was forgiven a 2 million dollar debt refusing to forgive the debt of someone who owed him $3!).

When word went back to the employer of how unforgiving his employee was, he restored the entire enormous debt. *"So also my heavenly Father will do to every one of you, if you do not forgive your brother from your heart."* (Matthew 18:35)

From this great parable we learn that forgiveness is not an option for the believer. In fact it is the primary responsibility of everyone who has received forgiveness. We pass that same forgiveness on to everyone. The way to continue living in the mercy, pardon and blessings of God is to keep passing it on to others. No matter how much people have hurt us, their offense towards us is nothing compared with the debt God has released us from.

The slightest unforgiveness towards self or others disturbs our peace with God and violates the principle of His mercy. Unforgiveness is like plaque in our arteries – it blocks the flow of God's love and life to us and through us.

We are all infinitely and equally in need of forgiveness. When we embrace the forgiveness that is in Jesus we have a special responsibility to show the same forgiveness to everyone else. A believer who leans on the mercy of God in Jesus and does not show total forgiveness towards others contradicts the principle of mercy on which his life is based.

Yes there are real things that others have done against us. There are people whose behavior we rightly don't like or whose views we rightly disagree with, but whether they are right or wrong, we still have an obligation to forgive. We do not have to condone people's wrong behavior or views but we do have an obligation to forgive and release them from any charge.

"For if you forgive men their trespasses, your heavenly Father also will forgive you; but if you do not forgive men their trespasses, neither will your Father forgive your trespasses." (Matthew 6:14-15)

TAKING OFFENSE

An offense is:

- an opportunity to forgive, or

- a temptation to unforgiveness

Jesus said *"Each day's trouble is enough for each day."* (Matthew 6:34) Each day brings along some offense or another. It can be as small as someone taking your parking space, annoying you with the noise of their radio, or as large as someone murdering a family member.

Believers can allow the law to take its course and to do its work to protect society from the evil that works through people. However, it is never right to harbor unforgiveness because when we take offence it cuts off the flow of God's further blessing and redeeming grace.

Forgiveness does not require that we agree with what has happened but that we refuse to let past misfortunes cut us off from present blessings.

"These things I have spoken to you," says *Jesus, "that my joy may be in you and that your joy may be full."* (John 15:11)

To the degree that we hold no unforgiveness towards self, God or others, we can live in the full sunshine of God's blessing.

IF ONLY!

The saddest phrase in our language is the phrase 'if only." It indicates regret over the past, and a failure to be released from its sorrow.

Unforgiveness is the glue that binds us to the past, and forgiveness is the liberation that enables us to embrace today's blessings. It is impossible to forgive, however, when those two little words "if only" bind us to our past. James says, *"We all make many mistakes."* (James 3:2) We have all been hurt in some way by our own mistakes and by the mistakes and injustices of others. This can become Satan's bait to enter into self-bitterness or bitterness towards others.

God, however, is our great Redeemer. He can take all the negatives in our lives and make them work for our good. When we give Him all our regrets, and receive His forgiveness for our sins, mistakes and failures, He looses us from our past.

We do not have to remain victims of our past, because Jesus, Our Redeemer, has the ability to make all things work for our good. *"And we know that all things work together for good to those who love God, to those who are called according to His purpose."* (Romans 8:28)

Unforgiveness is the glue that binds us to the past, and forgiveness is
the liberation that enables us to
embrace today's blessings.

When we release the pains, sorrows, disadvantages and injustices of our lives to Him, He, by His redemptive touch, makes it better that the bad things happened than if they had never happened. Adversity can be our prison house that locks us to the past, or it can be our stepping-stones to destiny. When we turn our adversities and disappointments over to the Lord our Redeemer, His Redemptive and Resurrection power seize the situation and forge destiny from it.

Most of the greatest leaders of history from Joseph to Martin Luther King have been schooled in the college of injustice and adversity. Those hardships handled with grace became the springboard to their destiny and influence.

Richard Wurmbrand, the writer of the autobiographic book "Tortured for Christ", was imprisoned in Romania first by the Nazis for being a Jew and then by communists for being a believer. In prison, he learned through the strengthening power of the Holy Spirit to endure, to forgive and to overcome. His experiences of persecution equipped him to become one of the most inspirational leaders of his time and the founder of "The Voice of the Martyrs', the leading ministry to the persecuted church.

FORGIVENESS IS NOT DENIAL

Forgiveness is not denial or brushing something under the carpet. True forgiveness faces the hurt and pain without diminishing its evil. Forgiveness is never a cover-up or hiding of problems from the light. On the contrary, it requires bringing everything into the light of truth and then covering it with love and forgiveness.

When we receive forgiveness from God we acknowledge our offense and receive pardon and restoration from God. Similarly, when we forgive others we do not diminish the offense but, fully acknowledging the seriousness of the offense, we forgive as we ourselves have been forgiven. The victim of rape, for example, should never be required to diminish or make little of the offense that has been perpetrated against her. On the contrary, only when she fully faces the depth of the violation can she fully forgive in a way that releases her from the offense and opens the door for healing and enlargement.

FOUR STEPS TO TOTAL FORGIVENESS

- Acknowledge the reality of the pain and suffering the offense of others has caused us.

- Forgive others of any real or imagined offense

- Release them from any sense of obligation to us arising from the offense just as Jesus has justified us and treats us as if we have never sinned

- Bless them. Just as God is never going to get back at you because He already 'got back' at Jesus for all our sins and trespasses, so we forgive others not to "get back" at them but that they will be blessed.

THE PHYSICAL EFFECTS OF UNFORGIVENESS

"Follow peace with all, and holiness, without which no one shall see the Lord; looking diligently lest any fail of the grace of God, or lest any root of

bitterness springing up disturb you, and by it many are defiled." (Hebrews 12:14-15)

A root of bitterness is literally a poisonous root. Medical science recognizes that emotions such as anger, guilt, sadness and resentment can damage our bodies and our mind. When negative emotions become chronic, they become literally poisonous, as they cause the body to produce excess doses of cortisol, histamines and other chemicals.

In addition to the obvious damage unforgiveness does to relationships, it can have a devastating effect on our physical health. According to Judith Perlman of the cancer Wellness Center of Suburban Chicago, "lack of forgiveness can create an avalanche of stress hormones." It increases production of cortisol and epinephrine, which leads to changes in heart rate and blood pressure. It raises levels of catecholamine and CD8, which suppresses the immune system thus increasing the risk of viral infection. It leads to the release of histamines, which can trigger severe broncho-constriction in people with asthma. Lack of forgiveness:

- alters insulin levels
- alters the acid concentration in the stomach
- causes plaque buildup in the arteries
- causes or intensifies aches and pains

- raises anxiety levels
- causes depression
- interferes with intimate and social relationships
- affects sleep and appetite

It is no wonder that Jesus said that we must forgive before we get on with any spiritual or any other life activity.

"And when you stand praying, if you have anything against anyone, forgive it so that also your Father in Heaven may forgive you your trespasses." (Mark 11:25)

WHO TO FORGIVE?

Unforgiveness is not only physically poisonous, it is also spiritually poisonous because it destroys relationships. In this way it undermines the basic fabric of life. Since we are created to receive and give love, unforgiveness destroys the most essential element of life.

Many find it hard to forgive because they themselves have never received it. They still believe that forgiveness has to be earned because of a false theology that God's mercy must be earned. However, the basis of Christian belief is that God loved us and provided atonement for our sins 'when we were still sinners.'

> When such as I cast out remorse,
> So great a sweetness flows into the breast,
> We must laugh, we must sing,
> We are blest,
> Everything we look upon is blest.
> – W.B. Yeats

"For we yet being without strength, in due time Christ died for the ungodly. For one will with difficulty die for a righteous one, yet perhaps one would even dare to die for a good one. But God commends His love toward us in that while we were yet sinners Christ died for us. Much more then, being now justified by His blood, we shall be saved from wrath through Him." (Romans 5:6-9)

If you believe you must somehow earn your forgiveness, then you will make other people earn their forgiveness also. But if you know you have not earned it you will more readily give it to others. Forgiveness is not earned; it is received. *"Freely you have received, freely give."* (Matthew 10:8)

The three great relationships for all of us are:

- our relationship with God
- our relationship with ourselves, and

- our relationship with others

Since forgiveness means we forgive the person of any real or imagined offense, we therefore extend forgiveness into those three great areas of relationships. We forgive:

- ourselves, for past failures and missed opportunities

- others, for all real and imagined offenses

- and God, for imagined offenses and for disappointments that we may have attributed to Him.

HOW OFTEN TO FORGIVE?

"Then Peter came up and said to him, 'Lord, how often shall my brother sin against me, and I forgive him? As many as seven times?'

Jesus answered *'Not seventy times but seventy times seven times"'* (Matt. 18:21-22)

Forgiveness is not something we occasionally do – a valve we sometimes turn on. It is a continuous flow towards everyone and every situation we meet. It is a lifestyle of mercy from ones who have received mercy. It is a habit of the most supernaturally empowered believers that keeps them connected with the love and joy of the Lord.

Jesus said *"Judge not, and you will not be judged; condemn not, and you will not be condemned; forgive, and you will be forgiven."* (Luke 6:37)

"For what is it to me to also judge those who are outside? Do you not judge those who are inside? But God judges those who are outside. Therefore put out from you the evil one." (1 Cor. 5:12-13)

At first sight these scriptures seem contradictory. Though we are warned not to judge, we also have the responsibility to discern and to take protective action in many situations to maintain good order. This kind of judgment and discernment is necessary.

What the Lord forbids is to "write someone off", despise them or esteem them as less than valuable because of their behavior or views. The only inhabitants of God's kingdom are pardoned sinners, and some of the greatest saints are those who have had the worst past. We may judge behavior but we may never judge people. This kind of judging is strictly limited to situations over which we have personal jurisdiction.

There is an apparent contradiction in the scriptures between the words of Jesus, *"Judge not that you may not be judged,"* (Matthew 7:1) and the words of Paul in 1 Corinthians 5. In fact there is no contradiction. The judgment Paul speaks of is not judging for condemnation but for correction, training and maintaining good order.

The exercise of forgiveness should never be taken as an excuse for not keeping good order. Leaders and rulers at every level have a responsibility to deal with wrong and illegal behavior. Such behavior has to be corrected for good order within society – in the home, in the congregations, and in public life. This is why we have a police and a court system. Imagine the chaos if we all ignored the traffic laws or if these laws were never enforced. So this kind of judging is absolutely necessary and the scriptures frequently sanction this good order. What they forbid is unforgiveness, bitterness and vengeance because of their toxic effect on us and on others.

> "I think, if God forgives,
> we must forgive ourselves.
> Otherwise it is almost like setting up ourselves
> as a higher tribunal than Him" – C. S. Lewis

'One of the primary characteristics of western society is an inability to enforce standards ... Laws do not mean much unless they are enforced. The saddest and most alarming trend is in the western churches … society has so influenced us that Yeshua's exhortation (judge not that you be not judged) has been taken to mean that we are not to enforce standards of righteousness in the Body of Believers.

The indulgent orientation of modern western Christianity also contradicts Paul's teaching in 1 Corinthians 5 and 6. Here we read that the community of faith is to discontinue fellowship with the sexually immoral members. Then we read that the community is to have a judiciary to settle serious disputes between members ... In many of today's churches … mercy and grace are perverted to allow license." (Excerpted from Dan Juster "Israel's Restoration" Jan 2008)

FORGIVENESS & ACCUSATION

Behind all unforgiveness is the spirit of the accuser - the devil. Accusation is his greatest strategy against believers. Accusation consists of thoughts bombarded into our consciousness from the realm of the spirit by evil spirits. These thoughts are designed to make us doubt:

- our salvation
- God's love for us and to
- hate ourselves, and
- hate others

Accusation is often directed at our own self-worth and provokes us to despise and hate others and ourselves. This can generate depression, despair, discouragement, self-loathing and even suicide. When accusation is directed towards others it produces envy, jealousy, bitterness and hatred.

Behind accusation are evil spirits whose master plan is to falsely accuse us. Therefore accusing thoughts have to be dealt with, not just with positive psychology but also by taking authority over lying thoughts and spirits. Since believers base their faith on the blood of Jesus and His atoning sacrifice, we know we are acceptable to God, not on the basis of our own performance, but on the basis of the perfect sacrifice of Jesus. We can, therefore, answer all accusations of the devil by pointing to the testimony of the blood of Jesus.

We can cancel all agreement with the accuser and come into agreement with the testimony of the Blood of Jesus. The testimony of the accuser is always: "You are guilty", "You are not good enough" The testimony of the blood of Jesus is, on the other hand, "You are forgiven", "Your sins are paid for", "You are acceptable in the Beloved."

In the light of this fact,
- we can refuse to agree with the negative thoughts of the accuser, and

- we can command the lying spirits behind those negative thoughts towards God, others and ourselves to flee in Jesus' name.

As we continue in this supernatural habit of forgiveness, the Holy Spirit will show us more areas where we can apply forgiveness to ourselves and others so that we can be released from every trace of guilt and bitterness. Many accusing thoughts are trapped in our consciousness for years, but once we recognize these thoughts are not in harmony with God and do not have their origin in Him, we can reject them from our consciousness and command the illegal spirits that have planted these thoughts to leave us.

Revelation 12:10 says that God's kingdom comes as the accuser is thrown down. *"And I heard a loud voice in heaven, saying, 'Now the salvation and the power and the kingdom of our God and the authority of his Christ have come, for the accuser of our brethren has been thrown down, who accuses them day and night before our God. And they have conquered him by the blood of the Lamb and by the word of their testimony, for they loved not their lives even unto death.'"* (Revelation 12:10-11)

The accuser has lost his legal right to accuse. When we forgive we continue in the realm of

God's kingdom of love and mercy but when we fail to forgive others we restore in part the realm of the accuser. The most supernaturally empowered believers know how to silence the voice of the accuser *"by the blood of the lamb and the word of our testimony."* (Revelation 12:11)

Forgiveness of self and others keeps the accuser dethroned and the wonderful realm of God's love, mercy and joy in the ascendancy every day.

This is the way of the supernaturally empowered believer.

CHAPTER 7

THE HABIT OF SELF- CONTROL

There are few areas where the difference between believers and the world around them is more obvious than in the area of sexual behavior and in the use of our bodies. .

The sexual standards of the kingdom of God are clear and simple. They are higher and more restrictive than the secular world, but they are also, as we shall see, highly liberating

The believer CHOOSES by an act of the will to live by standards revealed in the scriptures and renounces any other standards he may have lived by in the past. As he chooses to live by these values, he is immediately empowered by the Holy Spirit to live by them.

The supernaturally empowered believer lives by a moral code that differs greatly from the world around him. It is not because he has decided to become priggishly self-righteous, but because he has a new nature. His Adamic nature, which was bound to sinful behavior, has been replaced by the Nature of

Christ. As a new creature in Christ - he is empowered by the Spirit to live by a standard higher than his old nature was capable of.

The standards of God - which confine sexual intimacy to the relationship between one man and one woman in covenant and committed marriage - are far different than today's cultural norm. The believer's standards differ from the social norm of today's society - they are an alternative and totally different lifestyle. As Paul writes *"do not be conformed to his world but be transformed by the renewal of your minds that you may discover what is the good acceptable and perfect will of God. "* (Romans 12:2) The supernaturally empowered believer is a non-conformist. His values and lifestyle are strongly different from the values and ways of the world around him.

TOTAL FORGIVENESS BUT NO COMPROMISE

According to Scripture God's forgiveness is continually available when we fail to live by His high standards, but at the same time He is never permissive and never condones anything less than these standards.

Some of Jesus' followers complained that His standards were more demanding than the Law of Moses. He simply stated that God's original standard was for the man and woman to live in faithful loyalty towards each other. (Matt. 19:8-11) The intimacy of sex was reserved only to this special committed relationship. The aim was to create a special bond of closeness and love between the couple, resulting in children being born into secure loving and stable homes.

While upholding these high standards Jesus offers continuous forgiveness and release from guilt and condemnation to those who fail. To the woman caught in adultery. He said, *"Has no one condemned you? Neither do I - GO AND SIN NO MORE."* (John 8:11) He offered no condemnation. He extended no permissiveness but released her from the weight of guilt and condemnation while empowering her to walk away from the sin.

Jesus' method is not to condemn.

Neither is it to condone.

His method is **to forgive and transform.**

Strict legalism knows only condemnation. Strict permissiveness knows only to condone. God's way is to forgive and transform.

RELEASE FROM THE PENALTY & POWER OF SIN

Jesus releases us from the penalty of sin by His death for us and releases us from the power of sin by imparting His sinless resurrection life into us.

Though we have received a new nature victory over sexual sin and other sins of the body such as drunkenness and gluttony is not automatic. While sin has lost its dominion over us, we must now take dominion over it by

(1)   Firstly renouncing and resisting it,

(2)   Secondly drawing on the life of the resurrection to rise up in us against it i.e. for Jesus the overcomer to come forth in us and

(3) Thirdly (when necessary) command any evil - illegal spirit (especially one that has had access to us through our past behavior and history) to leave in Jesus' name.

GIVING OUR BODIES

"For just as you presented your members as slaves of uncleanness, and of lawlessness leading to more lawlessness, so now present your members as slaves off righteousness for holiness.

For when you were slaves of sin, you were free in regard to righteousness. What fruit did you have then in the things of which you are now ashamed? For the end of those things is death. But now having been set free from sin, and having become slaves of God, you have your fruit to holiness, and the end, everlasting life. (Romans 6:19-22)

Here Paul urges the believer to refuse to allow the sin to control him any more We are to 'present' i.e. give our bodies with all its parts to be instruments of righteousness.

In the past the believer may have abused his body by drug abuse, eating excessively, sexual promiscuity, etc. Now he is exhorted to cease from any wrong uses of his body, mind and words and deliberately CHOOSE to make his body an instrument of righteousness.

This is more than mere self-righteous good resolution, - it is a deliberate CHOICE he can now make because his old sinful nature has been crucified (executed) with Christ and he has a new nature. It is a CHOICE that relies on the energizing power of the righteous resurrection life of the spirit of Jesus now living in him.

JUSTIFICATION & SUBSEQUENT BEHAVIOR

The Bible is clear: no one is justified by their moral behavior - because no one is without sin. We all stand guilty. Jesus paid for the sin of every one of us. Upon faith in this fact and a sincere desire to be reconciled with God we are justified and restored into right standing with Him and to his favor and blessing.

Because this restoration is offered to us in spite of our failed behavior, some have concluded that our behavior after salvation is not important. However Paul, the great proclaimer of justification as a gift, was also careful to point out that the believer is expected to shake off the sinful patterns of his old ways and to put on the upright and gracious ways of Jesus. He now has the ability to remove sexual immorality, gluttony, drug and alcohol abuse from his life because they are incompatible with the new nature.

Neither sexual sin nor any other sin can be overcome by placing people under guilt - but by releasing them from guilt and connecting them to the life of the Spirit of God. However, release from guilt does not mean release from standards.

Paul writes, *"For in Christ Jesus the law of the Spirit of life has set you free from the law of sin and death. For the Law was powerless to do , in that it was weakened by the flesh God did by sending His own Son in likeness of sinful man, as an offering for sin. He thus condemned sin in the flesh, so that the righteous standard of the Law might be fulfilled in us, who do not live according to the flesh but according to the Spirit* (Romans 8:2-4)

The moral health that the Law sought to legislate comes to us when we receive the spiritual moral health of Jesus. The law was powerless to bring moral health it only brought guilt. It standards were good but its methods were powerless.

A NEW WAY OF LIVING

> "Nothing has stolen more dreams, dashed more hopes, broken up more families, and messed up more people psychologically than our propensity to disregard God's commands regarding sexual purity."   -Andy Stanley

The believer's way is a new supernatural way of living. In the days of the early church (just like today) many of the believers were coming from backgrounds of sexual immorality. Through faith in Jesus the stain and record of past wrongdoing was erased from

their record and through the new life they were empowered to live lives of sexual cleanness and self-control. Remember: *"Every saint has a past and every sinner has a future."*

God promised that He would remove the corrupt part of our nature - the adamic nature and replace it with His Spirit. *"Then I will sprinkle clean water on you, and you will be clean; I will cleanse you from all your filthiness and from all your idols."* (Ezekiel 36:25) God not only forgives - He cleanses us and transforms us, if we choose to cooperate with His ways and receive His supernatural life.

"Therefore consider the members of your earthly body as dead to immorality, impurity, passion, evil desire, and greed, which amounts to idolatry." (**Colossians 3:5**)

"Flee from sexual immorality. All other sins a person commits are outside the body, but whoever sins sexually, sins against their own body. " (1 Cor. 6:18)

"For this is the will of God, your sanctification; that is, that you abstain from sexual immorality." (1 Thess. 4:3)

HIGH COST OF IGNORING THIS HABIT

Family structure and poverty are intertwined. According to data published by ASHA (The American Sexual Health Association) nearly a third of households in the U.S. headed by single women live below the poverty line compared to only six percent of households headed by married couples. Poverty, meanwhile, touches an astounding **45 percent of children** who live without a father. (Emily Badger)

- More than half of all people will have an STD/STI (Sexually transmitted diseases and

- infections) at some point in their lifetime.
- There are 19.7 million new STIs every year in the U.S.
- In 2008, there were an estimated 110 million prevalent STIs among women and men in the U.S. Of these, more than 20% (22.1 million) were among women and men aged 15 to 24 years.
- The total estimated direct cost of STIs annually in the U.S. is $15.6 billion (2010 US dollars).
- Each year, one in four teens contracts an STD/STI.
- One in two sexually active persons will contract an STD/STI by age 25.
- About half of all new STDs/STIs in 2000 occurred among youth ages 15 to 24.[7] The total estimated costs of these nine million new cases of these STDs/STIs was $6.5 billion, with HIV and human papillomavirus (HPV) accounting for 90% of the total burden.
- Of the STDs/STIs that are diagnosed, only some (gonorrhea, syphilis, chlamydia, hepatitis A and B) are required.

All these statistics create a 'misery index', which clearly shows that so called 'sexual freedom' is far from liberating. It takes a huge toll on the physical and psychological well being of this generation. There is a high cost for not choosing the supernatural habit of self-control. This is not to mention the immense psychological toll taken by the rejection and loss of self-esteem caused by broken relationships.

An unintended consequence of sexual liberty is of course unwanted and unforeseen pregnancies. In the West this amounts to the death of 25% of all pregnancies. No one can measure the lost potential of those human lives. No one can measure the hidden guilt and pain which the majority of those mothers experience and the damage of this guilt to their psyches. The hidden sadness - the lost lives and the social, physical and financial cost of those lives, are beyond measure and the result of bad choices.

OTHER FACETS OF SELF- CONTROL

*"But **the fruit of the Spirit** is love, joy, peace, forbearance, kindness, goodness, faithfulness, gentleness and self-control."* (Galatians 2:23)

Self- control is part of the fruit of the spirit. It is the ability to rule over our temper, tongue and bodies. The Holy Spirit empowers us with self-control and with His help we can avoid self-destructive uses of our bodies.

We have focused primarily in this chapter on the problems we create for ourselves by our failure to rule over our sex-lives. The problems we create for ourselves by our inability to control our other appetites are also huge. The health and social costs of alcohol and drug abuse are incalculable. The self-harm and pain caused to families by food, alcohol and drug abuse are also enormous. They are some of the principle causes of poverty.

CONCLUSION

THE WAY OF THE WISE

Our Loving Heavenly Father calls us through His Word and through His Son to flee the ways of foolishness that lead to misery and embrace the ways of wisdom that leads to abundant life.

Blessed is the man
Who walks not in the counsel of the ungodly,
Nor stands in the path of sinners,
Nor sits in the seat of the scornful;
² But his delight is in the law of the Lord,
And in His law he meditates day and night.
³ He shall be like a tree
Planted by the rivers of water,
That brings forth its fruit in its season,
Whose leaf also shall not wither;
And whatever he does shall prosper. (Psalm 1)

The supernatural habit of self-control is the way of wisdom. Wisdom is the ability to use knowledge and resources in ways that advance our own happiness, well-being and the happiness and well-being of others. Unbridled by wisdom our lives collapse into misery, but when directed by wisdom they become joyful and fruitful.

The scriptures frequently contrast wisdom and foolishness. They warn against foolishness and encourage us towards wisdom. Wisdom cries out to us to follow its ways. God is crying out to humanity to turn away from the ways of foolishness and to learn from Him the ways of wisdom.

"Wisdom calls aloud outside; she raises her voice in the open squares. She speaks her words: "How long, you simple ones, will you love simplicity? But whoever listens to me will dwell safely, and will be secure, without fear of evil." (Prov. 1:20,22,23)

"Therefore everyone who hears these words of mine and puts them into practice is like a wise man who built his house on the rock." (Matt. 7.24)

The supernaturally empowered believer has chosen the ways of WISDOM. As a follower of Jesus and His ways, he cultivates the supernatural habit of self-control. It is a decision to live by God's standards and it is one of the great keys of abundant living.

CHAPTER 7

THE HABIT OF SPEAKING LIFE

Examine the following statements:

I Love you	*I hate you.*
You're beautiful.	*You're ugly.*
You're a blessing.	*You never do anything right.*
Thank you. That's great!	*It's all you fault*
I enjoyed that.	*That could have been better.*
You'll make it.	*You'll never be good at that.*
We're proud of you.	*You're a disappointment to us.*
I'm blessed with great health.	*At my age what can you expect*

Each of these statements does not simply carry information but conveys emotion. The emotion conveyed in these simple statements can either build someone up or destroy them. Our minds are like a river where streams of words and thoughts flow continually. The words we agree with and store up in our souls will determine our destiny. Our spoken words establish agreement or disagreement with our thoughts and seal them into our consciousness and lives. It is, therefore, vital to our well-being and destiny that we learn to use our tongues effectively, and to carefully choose what thoughts we establish and reinforce with our tongues.

Therefore one of the most essential elements of supernatural living is the use of the tongue. The most effective productive and joyful believers learn to use their tongues in positive, merciful and kindly ways. We are promised that if we do this we will see good days and long life. *"For he that wants to love life and to see good days, let him restrain his tongue from evil, and his lips from speaking guile."* (1 Peter 3:10)

Traditional Christianity and Judaism have paid insufficient attention to this vital part of life. Our words have a much more important part to play in the effectiveness, success and quality of our lives than most people realize.

WORDS & DOMINION
When God first made man (male and female)

female) He gave them dominion over all the creatures on the earth. They exercised their dominion primarily by their use of words. *"And God said, 'Let us make man in our image, after our likeness. And let them have dominion over the fish of the sea, and over the fowl of the heavens, and over the cattle, and over all the earth, and over all the creepers creeping on the earth.'"* (Genesis 1:26) Adam exercised this dominion by using his tongue to name the animals.

We exercise dominion over our lives through the use of the tongue along with our prayers, faith, thoughts and actions.

Throughout His teachings Jesus emphasized the redeemed use of the tongue, and He modeled it in His actions.

"A good man out of the good treasure of the heart brings out good things; and an evil man out of the evil treasure brings out evil things. But I say to you that every idle word, whatever men may speak, they shall give account of it in the Day of Judgment. For by your words you shall be justified, and by your words you shall be condemned." (Matt. 12:35-37)

Here Jesus says that our tongues will actually decide our present and eternal destiny.

How can this be? Most Christians believe that faith and behavior determine our destiny. This is true, but our tongues have an equally important part in determining our destiny as with them we engage our wills and give our consent.

EMBRACING DESTINY WITH WORDS

God has provided atonement for every human being through the death of Jesus on the Cross-. Our part is to receive this reconciliation by faith and repentance and to be reconciled with God. But it is with our words (and not just with our minds) that we establish and seal our acceptance of God's free gift and plan. With our mouth we declare that Christ's death has sufficiently paid for our sin and with it we accept the reconciliation. We seal legal transactions with our written signature. We seal spiritual transactions with our spoken words. Our verbal agreement or disagreement seals our covenant with God. That is why Christianity is called "the great confession" (see Hebrews 4:14).

The tongue is the key to the release of our faith in God's settled fact.
Through it we establish agreement with God's plan or reject it.

"Because if you confess the Lord Jesus, and believe in your heart that God has raised Him from the dead, you shall be saved. For with the heart one believes unto righteousness, and with the mouth one confesses unto salvation." (Romans 10:9-10) The tongue is the key to the release of our faith in God's settled fact. Through it we establish agreement with God's plan or reject it.

There are many today who agree with the doctrines of Christianity (believe that Jesus is the Son of God and Savior who died and rose for the sins of the world etc.) but who have never released their faith in these great realities with their tongues. They believe in the reality of salvation but have never fully embraced it by the commitment of their wills and their tongue. They have never embraced the assurance of their salvation because they have never confessed with their mouths Jesus as Savior and Lord. They are like couples that have never formalized their union by saying, "I do."

WORDS DECIDE BUT DO NOT CREATE DESTINY

Our words decide destiny. They do not create our destiny, but they are the key to embracing God's destiny for our lives. There are some who try to create their future with their words. This is a kind of psychological witchcraft, which involves the use of the mind more than the spirit. It is more metaphysical than spiritual. It harnesses the laws of quantum physics more than the power of God.

The supernaturally empowered believer does not try to create his destiny with his tongue but he does use his tongue to express his agreement and assent to the Word of God. With our words we establish the Word of God and the plan of God in our lives. With them we can also reject recurring thoughts that could derail or steal our destiny. *"The thief comes to steal kill and destroy but I am come that you might have life and have it more abundantly."* (John 10:10)

THE TONGUE & THE MIND

Our tongues determine what will remain our consciousness. Our consciousness determines the outcome of our lives. Paul writes, *"Be transformed by the renewal of your minds."* (Romans 12:2) How do we do this? By ejecting old thought forms from our consciousness and filling our minds with the thoughts of the kingdom of God, thoughts that are in line with the Word of God.

"Finally, brethren, whatever is true, whatever is honorable, whatever is just, whatever is pure, whatever is lovely, whatever is gracious, if there is

any excellence, if there is anything worthy of praise, think about these things. What you have learned and received and heard and seen in me, do; and the God of peace will be with you." (Philippians 4:8-9)

So we have the responsibility to resist and reject thoughts from the kingdom of darkness that would derail us from the benign plan and will of God for our lives.

Let's examine the words in our columns again.

I Love you	I hate you.
You're beautiful.	You're ugly.
You're a blessing.	You never do anything right.
Thank you. That's great!	It's all you fault
I enjoyed that.	That could have been better.
You'll make it.	You'll never be good at that.
We're proud of you.	You're disappointment to us.
I'm blessed with great health.	At my age what can you expect

If the words in the first column are spoken over me, my agreement with them will affirm and help establish the good things in my life. The second column contains words of accusation. If I agree with them I orientate myself to that which steals my confidence, love and joy and ultimately my health. I will begin to say things about myself such as "I am no good", "I will never be able to do this or that", "God does not really love me", "I hate myself", "I am a failure" etc. etc. One set of words will strengthen me emotionally and the other set will tear me down.

OUR WORDS & GOD'S WORD

Now if our agreement with simply human words of affirmation can have such a positive effect on us, what will happen when we agree with the Word of God and the promises of God?

Agreement with positive words aligns our minds in a positive way; but agreeing with the Word of God opens a channel for the release of God's plan into our lives. Both are good; but one is temporary and the other is eternal. Because God has given us free-will He does not force His will on us. Our agreement with the Word of God releases Him to do what He has chosen not to do without our willing assent. Our words express our free exercise of will and with them we release our consent and embrace His will.

The Bible contains hundreds of promises from God for those who enter covenant with Him. For example, *"I am the Lord who blots out your offenses"* (Isaiah 43:25), *"The Lord has laid on Him the iniquity of us all"* (Isaiah 53:6), *"He who comes to me I will in no way cast out"* (John 6:37), *"All things work together for good for those who love God who are called according to his purpose"* (Romans 8:28), and *"I know the plans I have for you, plans for your welfare and not for your harm to give you a hope and a future"* (Jeremiah 29:11).

In fact there are promises in the Word of God that cover every area of human need. When we live in a reconciled relationship with God through the atoning work of Jesus we can ask Him to fulfill these promises for us.

As we read and study these promises, faith arises in our hearts, because *"faith comes by hearing and hearing by the Word of God."* (Romans 10:17) When we release our faith with our words God comes on the scene. He looks for people who will come into agreement with His word and promises. This releases His intervention in our lives.

"For the eyes of the Lord are on the righteous, and His ears open to their prayers. But the Lord's face is against those who do evil." (1 Peter 3:12)

"For the eyes of the LORD run to and fro throughout the whole earth, to show his might in behalf of those whose heart is blameless toward him. You have done foolishly in this; for from now on you will have wars." (2 Chron. 16:9)

"For I will watch over My word to perform it." (Jeremiah 1:12)

As God watches over His word to perform it the believer begins to harness the supernatural power of speaking in line with this word. Words are the switch that releases the power of God into our situations.

One of the greatest examples of this is found in the announcement of God's word to Mary, the virgin of Nazareth that she was chosen to be the mother of the Messiah. God announced His plan through the angel Gabriel. She uttered her assent: *"Be it done to me according to your word."* (Luke 1:38) This response of Mary is a spectacular example of the use of words to embrace and release the plan of God.

USING WORDS TO RESIST THE DEVIL

Jesus defeated the devil in the wilderness by refusing to come into agreement with the thoughts that he sought to inject into His consciousness. Jesus recognized Satan as the source of these thoughts and refused to agree with them. He then commanded the evil spirit (Satan) that was transmitting them to leave (Luke 4:12).

Since we live in a universe inhabited by many spirits (including spirits that are in rebellion to God) we have to deal with evil spirits. Many people do not like to deal with spirits. The supernatural believer knows that he lives in a world where there are many evil spirits working in the unseen realm. These spirits generate confusion and fear.

However, the supernaturally empowered believer knows he has authority over sin and over the spirits that try to oppress him. He takes seriously the words of Jesus: *"Behold, I give you authority to tread on serpents and scorpions, and over all the authority of the enemy. And nothing shall by any means hurt you."* (Luke 10:19)

"And these signs shall accompany them that believe: in my name shall they expel demons..." (Mark 16:17)

Evil spirits operate by trying to speak thoughts, fantasies and imaginations into us. Our task is to recognize the lie, refuse to agree with it, and then resist the spirit behind the lie.

"Believe not every spirit but test the spirits." (1 John 4:1) We can test the spirits by checking if their suggestion lines up with the word of and ways of God or not. If they do not, we simply resist them.

"Resist the devil and he will flee from you." (James 4:7) The devil and the evil spirits that work under his rule have lost their authority over us. However, they try to re-establish their authority over us by tempting us to agree with their thoughts, lies and suggestions. Knowing that Jesus has defeated them we can refuse to come into agreement with the thoughts they transmit and take the authority He has given us to command them to flee.

> "Men should utter nothing for which they would not willingly be responsible through time and in eternity"
> – Abraham Lincoln

For example, demons may transmit unclean thoughts or suicidal thoughts to believers especially if we have given ground to such thoughts through past behavior. The supernatural empowered believer can:

- recognize that such thoughts are not from God

- cancel any agreement we have made with these thoughts, and

- command the spirits that are transmitting these thoughts to leave in Jesus' name

TRAINING OUR TONGUES

We can train our tongues to become effective instruments to steer our lives in the direction of God. Because our speech patterns were formed before Christ came into our hearts, we have to retrain them.

James actually says that if we learn to use our tongues properly we will be mature believers. He explains that as a ship is steered by a rudder we steer our lives by our tongues. As a horse is steered by a bit, God can only steer us through our mouths.

"If anyone does not offend in word, the same is a full-grown man, able also to bridle the whole body. Behold, we put bits in the horses' mouths, so that they may obey us, and we turn about their whole body. Behold also the ships being so great, and driven by fierce winds, yet they are turned about with a very small rudder, where the impulse of him steering desires." (James 3:2-4)

Even the most casual words have an effect on our lives. Our words are seeds, which determine our future. *"Death and life are in the power of the tongue, and those who love it will eat its fruits."* (Proverbs 18:21)

What could be more important than learning how to use our tongues properly? Children are taught how to develop and use their minds but not how to use their tongues.

Our culture does not sufficiently emphasize the use of the tongue and children receive very little education on the proper use of the tongue. Right use of the tongue is much more than being polite and pronouncing our words properly. By learning to use our tongues properly we are learning to use the steering wheel of our destiny. To educate people without teaching them about the tongue is like teaching road rules without teaching how to use the steering wheel. This right use of the tongue is the key to embracing the promises and destiny of God and to keeping ourselves aligned with His purposes.

BLESSING & CURSING

The New Testament instructs the supernaturally empowered believer on the importance and power of the tongue. James says

"Even so the tongue is a little member and boasts great things. But no one can tame the tongue; it is an unruly evil, full of deadly poison. By this we bless God, even the Father. And by this we curse men, who have come into being according to the image of God. Out of the same mouth proceeds blessing and cursing. My brothers, these things ought not to be so." (James 3:5-10)

He urges believers not to permit negative, bitter or cursed words from our mouths because they are consecrated to speak forth the praises and blessings of God.

People usually think of cursing as unclean language and expletives but it is much more than that. To curse is to pronounce negative words on ourselves, others or on situations. A curse brings us into agreement with the negative it pronounces and creates a highway for the evil one's negative plot. To bless means to speak forth positive and hopeful words on ourselves, others and our situations in line with God's revealed plan and benign attitude. Blessing creates a highway for God's benign plan.

James says, *"No man can tame the tongue."* (James 3:8) However, the Holy Spirit can tame our tongues when we surrender them to Him. Our tongues are not only connected to our minds, they are also directly connected to our hearts. Through the tongue we can control what we permit to lodge in our hearts. Through it we can direct what goes into our hearts. Truth does not reach the heart until it is placed in the mouth. As food goes from the mouth to the stomach and then to the blood, spiritual truth goes from our mouths to our hearts and then throughout our lifestream where it translates into energy. The heart renews the tongue and the tongue renews the heart.

The dynamic connection between the heart of man and his spirit is one of the reasons that speaking in the heavenly language is such a vital and life-giving blessing for supernaturally empowered believers.

With the new heart of love that comes from the Holy Spirit we can train our tongues to speak love and only love, blessing and only blessing. Effective disciples learn to put cursing away from their mouths and to bless everything about themselves and others. This is a faith discipline that enables us to remain in abiding union with God's benign plan. *"Speaking the truth in love, we grow up in all things, to Him who is the Head, even Christ."* (Ephesians 4:15) As we speak in this way we are maturing to become more like Jesus.

If we have cursed ourselves, our situations or others in the past we can ask the Lord's forgiveness, cancel the agreement we made with the negative, and begin to bless ourselves, our situations and others. We can use the blessing to undo the effect of the curse.

USING OUR TONGUES TO RULE & DECREE

Our tongues, as we have seen, can be used

in prayer, in coming into agreement with God's plan, and in rejecting any other plans or directions of our lives out of line with God's highest and best for us or others.

We can also use our tongues to speak forth the plan of God and to speak against natural forces, illegal spirits and even inanimate objects that hinder the plan and purposes of God.

"You shall also decree a thing, and it shall be established for you: and the light shall shine upon your ways." (Job 22:28)

"For truly I say to you that whoever shall say to this mountain, 'Be moved and be cast into the sea', and shall not doubt in his heart, but shall believe that what he said shall occur, he shall have whatever he said. Therefore I say to you, all things, whatever you ask, praying, believe that you shall receive them, and it will be to you. And when you stand praying, if you have anything against anyone, forgive it so that also your Father in Heaven may forgive you your trespasses. But if you do not forgive, neither will your Father in Heaven forgive your trespasses." (Mark 11:23-26)

Before we use the prayer of authority, command and decree, we should first ascertain that this situation is not a providential circumstance, permitted so that we can overcome evil with good.

If we attempt to rebuke situations that God has providentially permitted for our growth we will fail to overcome. The authoritative use of our words requires that we be without unforgiveness, anger or bitterness towards anyone. It is unthinkable for a Christian to try to harm others with negative words.

However, there are occasionally demonically engineered circumstances, where it is appropriate to take dominion and speak words of command over the illegal spirits operating in the circumstance. In these cases we can speak forth in prayers of authority against obstacles that hinder the will of God in our spheres of responsibility and influence.

WORDS KEEP THE SPIRIT'S LIFE ACTIVE IN US

"Be filled with the spirit speaking to yourselves in psalms and hymns and spiritual songs, singing and making melody in your heart to the Lord." (Eph. 5: 19)

Here Paul urges us to use our tongues to continuously speak the praises of God and celebrate His goodness. This keeps us built up in the Lord and the life of the Spirit flowing in our hearts and lives. This kind of wholehearted praise connects us in such a vital way with the throne of God that it releases the operation of His miraculous power and the activity of His angels.

We see this in Paul's life, when on one occasion after he and Silas had been severely beaten and locked in jail they began to praise God loudly at midnight. As they did this God sent an angel to unlock the prison doors and Paul won the jailer to Christ.

"But about midnight Paul and Silas were praying and singing hymns unto God, and the prisoners were listening to them; and suddenly there was a great earthquake, so that the foundations of the prison-house were shaken: and immediately all the doors were opened, and every one's bands were loosed." (Acts 16:25-26)

A similar story is recounted in Chronicles when Judah was invaded by a vastly superior coalition of three armies in the days of Jehosophat. Though vastly outnumbered Jehosophat began to look to God and sent out choirs praising God before the army. As they did this, God released the angelic hosts to overcome and confuse the enemies of Judah.

"And when he had taken counsel with the people, he appointed those who were to sing to the LORD and praise him in holy array, as they went before the army, and say, 'Give thanks to the LORD, for his steadfast love endures for ever.'

And when they began to sing and praise, the LORD set an ambush against the men of Ammon,

133

Moab, and Mount Seir, who had come against Judah, so that they were routed." (2 Chronicles 20:21-22)

Praise releases the power of God into our situations. On the other hand, negative fear-filled and complaining words quench and dampen the life of the Spirit within us. When we turn the switch of the tongue from whining and complaining to praising and thanksgiving we hook up with the supernatural power of God, and heaven breaks in.

THE HEAVENLY LANGUAGE

No discussion of the supernaturally empowered believer's use of the tongue would be complete without mentioning the "gift of tongues" so often referred to in the New Testament writings.

"And these signs will accompany those who believe: in my name they will cast out demons; they will speak in new tongues..." (Mark 16:17)

"And they were all filled with the Holy Spirit and began to speak in other tongues, as the Spirit gave them utterance." (Acts 2:4)

"Now I want you all to speak in tongues but even more to prophecy." (1 Cor. 14.5)

"But you, beloved, building yourselves up by your most holy faith, praying in the Holy Spirit, keep yourselves in the love of God, eagerly

134

awaiting the mercy of our Lord Jesus Christ to everlasting life." (Jude 1:20-21)

The supernaturally empowered believer knows how to use his tongue in the heavenly prayer language. This language enables him to pray beyond the limits of his mind and intellect.

The heavenly prayer language is one of the greatest tools of the spiritual believer as through it we can pray beyond the limits of the understanding. It opens a way for the wisdom of heaven, which is superior to natural wisdom, to flow through our hearts. When we pray in our own language we voice the concerns of our minds and pray about matters we are aware of. When we pray in tongues, on the other hand, we pray in mysteries that are beyond the reach of the intellect.

God has made this gift available to all supernaturally empowered believers as a means of recharging our spirits. It is unfortunate that this link between our spirit and the unseen realm has been neglected by so many. The most supernaturally empowered believers of the ages have known the importance of this tremendous supernatural resource.

CHAPTER 8

THE HABIT OF SERVING/MINISTRY

The supernaturally empowered believer is a servant through and through. They know that God who saved us, not by our own works, has sent them out to do good works. *"We are God's workmanship created in Christ Jesus for good works that we should walk in them."* (Ephesians 2:10) These good works are not just any acts of service but works, which have been supernaturally set up by God through which we serve and advance His kingdom.

SERVING IN TWO DIRECTIONS

Everyone will serve something: self, idols, money or dead works. Believers have been rescued from slavery in empty, dead and futile works to serve the living God.

Believers see themselves firstly as servants of God and then as servants of others as God directs. A servant is one who seeks the Master's will above everything. His delight and only responsibility is to do the Master's will. *"You shall worship the Lord your God, and Him only shall you serve."* (Mt. 4:10)

Believers serve in two directions:

- upwards towards God with thanksgiving, and
- outwards from God towards man in service.

Jesus said you *"cannot serve two masters; for either he will hate the one and love the other, or he will be devoted to the one and despise the other."* (Matthew 6:24)

"As they ministered to the Lord and fasted, the Holy Spirit said, 'So, then, separate Barnabas and Saul to Me for the work to which I have called them.'" (Acts 13:2)

When our focus is on God Himself rather than our work for Him, He can direct our work. When the focus is on work we miss his direction and flounder in a maze of human programs. Paul & Barnabas ministered to the Lord and in that place of intimacy with Him received their assignment. Ministry to the Lord in love and intimacy is the taproot of all supernatural service and real success. The work of the supernaturally empowered believer is qualitatively different from the work of a mere hired man. It uses natural energy and skills but it also is backed up by God's blessing and power. It comes not from the deadness of mere duty but from a heart of love and compassion. As Frances Roberts writes, *"For I do not ask you to labor in drudgery, but the work of God is a labor of love, for God is love; and as you live by the motivation of my Spirit, you shall be partaker continually of my life."* ("Come Away My Beloved" by Frances Roberts, p.112)

God does not merely ask us to serve - but to serve as directed by Him.
Our response is not primarily to need but to God who sends us to meet need.

Service to the world or to merely selfish ends ultimately brings disillusionment, heartbreak and disappointment. Service to the Lord, on the other hand, is sweet. Jesus said, *"Learn of me for I am meek and gentle and lowly of heart and you will find rest for your souls, for my yoke is easy and my burden light."* (Matthew 11:29) Serving Him brings a rest, joy and inner satisfaction that no other service can give.

SERVING GOD'S AGENDA NOT MAN'S

Jesus corrected religious people for putting burdens on others. Religion puts burdens on people and co-opts them to serve programs, plans and purposes to which they may not be called. These false burdens operate through psychological control and fear. They counterfeit the real service of the Lord. Supernaturally empowered believers are not pressurized by religious manipulation but serve in loving partnership with the Lord. It is tragic to spend years in religious service, thinking one is serving the Lord, when all we are doing is serving a religious spirit, a religious program, or the ambition of a denomination or leader. The gospel calls us out from obedience to yokes of slavery to the easy yoke of the Lord.

"For freedom Christ has set us free; stand fast therefore, and do not submit again to a yoke of slavery." (Galatians 5:1)

God may call nine people to serve in a certain way and the tenth person to do something completely different. Today there are many demands and pressures on believers from a world full of needs. God does not merely ask us to serve - but to serve as directed by Him. Our response is not primarily to need but to God who sends us to meet need. We are related to God first and He relates us to meet certain needs. One thing done FROM God is better than a thousand things done FOR God.

As believers we live from Heaven towards earth .... partnering with God as He directs us to bring His mercy to areas where He directs. He will direct each one in different ways. If we imitate and copy each other we miss God's direction for us. We can be challenged and inspired by each other but our acts must be directed from God. What has its origin in flesh – even in good flesh - is flesh, and what has its origin in spirit is spirit. *"That which is born of the flesh is flesh that which is born of the spirit is spirit."* (Jn. 3:6)

SERVICE & SACRIFICE

Sadly, service to the Lord is often presented as a great sacrifice. It is true that service of the Lord requires that we give up some things but this is true in the life of everyone who dedicates themselves to a cause. The athlete for example disciplines himself to attain his goal. The scientist dedicates his time in study to pursue his research.

As we dedicate ourselves to the Lord's goal for our lives and pursue our highest destiny, we give up everything worth losing for the sake of gaining everything worth keeping. We give up heaviness and put on joy. We give up selfishness and put on unselfishness. We give up indifference and pick up love. We give up isolation and we pick up friendship.

We give up dysfunctional and destructive habits and put on life-giving habits. *"He gives us beauty for ashes, the oil of joy for mourning and the garment of praise for the spirit of heaviness."* (Isaiah 61:3)

As Jesus says: *"he who loves his life must lose it and he who loses his life finds it."* (Matthew 10:39) This has often been misinterpreted to mean we must constantly repress ourselves, our feelings, thoughts, dreams and desires. Such repression of desire and feeling is more akin to Buddhism than true Christianity. What Jesus is saying is that if we are to really enter into God's plan and purposes – the abundance of the kingdom of God - we must place our lives on a new foundation. The self-built life must be replaced by a life that is built on the Creator's promises and purposes. Once we are surrendered and willingly subordinated to Him our dreams and desires come into harmony with Him.

There is no longer a dualism between our will and His and we begin to work with Him not just as servants but as His friends and partners. The dedication of the believer is never to any particular work or organization but to God Himself who directs his steps.

LIFE ON A NEW FOUNDATION

"And He said to them, 'Follow Me', and I

will make you fishers of men." (Matt. 4:19)

When the early disciples found the Messiah it ruined their appetite for every other form of service. They left their nets and followed Him. They had seen the kingdom of God. They had glimpsed God's plan to invade earth with his mercy and they gave themselves to Him to partner with Him in extending His mercy to the earth.

Not everyone is called to physically leave their nets. All will have a different relationship with their 'nets' when they find Him. The call of God is never to the ministry – the call is to follow Him and serve Him. What made their call holy was not that it was a call to 'ministry' but a call to set their lives on a whole new foundation. Instead of being self-directed they were to be God directed. Even their natural fishing became God-directed and when God-directed it became supernaturally successful and blessed.

Traditional Christianity has taught mistakenly that some are called to the ministry and others called to secular service. The truth is that all supernaturally effective believers are called to follow Jesus and to serve in different ways as He directs. Many dedicate themselves to work for a certain organization or denomination, but this falls short of Jesus' great call to us: 'Come follow Me.' Our dedication is not to the ministry or to "The

Church" but to Him.

"I beseech you therefore, brothers, by the mercies of God to present your bodies a living sacrifice, holy, pleasing to God, which is your reasonable service. And do not be conformed to this world, but be transformed by the renewing of your mind, in order to prove by you what is that good and pleasing and perfect will of God." (Romans 12: 1-2)

This passage has often been used as a call to martyr-like sacrifice. In fact it is a commonsense invitation to align with God's good plans and to be available to serve Him and His purposes. We can abandon the measuring rods, mindsets and goals of the world's system and give ourselves wholeheartedly to the purposes and plans He has for us.

The supernatural believer is drafted into a great revolution – the revolution of bringing heaven to earth. He is joined to God's plan and enterprise towards oppressed mankind:

- to reconcile them to Himself through the revelation of the cross

- to put a new spirit within them

- to break the curse imposed by ignorance and demonic oppression,

- and to bring His healing mercy to them.

We take our part with the Messiah in His eternal ministry.

"The Spirit of the Lord is upon me, because he has anointed me to preach good news to the poor. He has sent me to proclaim release to the captives and recovering of sight to the blind, to set at liberty those who are oppressed to proclaim the acceptable year of the Lord." (Luke 4:18-19; Isaiah 61:1-2)

As we serve God, He places us in the service of others. As the disciples ministered to the Lord in prayer and thanksgiving and listened for His direction, He directed Paul & Barnabas, to go to Antioch. This mission became the great breakthrough mission of the early church. All ministry and service should flow from our ministry to the Lord in praise and thanksgiving.

Receiving the proceeding word from the Lord is the key to effective service. When we serve without God's direction and without first ministering to Him, we become need driven and program driven rather than Spirit driven and we miss the supernatural blessing of God on the work.

One thing done from God is better than a thousand things done for God. Without the Lord's direction we are simply serving impulse, need, pressure or some other force than the Lord.

Christian work becomes lifeless and disintegrates into ritual and imitation.

SERVICE & IDENTITY

"Beloved, now we are children of God, and it has not yet been revealed what we shall be. But we know that when He shall be revealed, we shall be like Him, for we shall see Him as He is." (1 John 3:2)

The New Testament scriptures proclaim exuberantly in various ways the facets and glory of our new identity in Christ. We are *"redeemed"*, *"adopted"* into God's family, *"partakers of the divine nature"*, *"children of God"*, *"blessed in all things"*, and *"kings and priests to the Lord."* (Eph. 1:8, Gal. 4:5; 2 Pt. 1:4; Rom. 8:16; Eph.1:3; Rev. 1:6)

This is the amazing new identity of the believer in Jesus. With such a fabulous identity in Christ we do not have to look to our career or our position in the world or the church for our identity.

Jesus "knowing who He was… took a towel." When we really know who we are, we will not be afraid of humble and obscure service. We will be less tempted to abuse ministry by using it as a vehicle for our status or identity. When we do not have to work to prove we are something or somebody, we can cease from our drivenness and striving. Our doing comes from our being. We can now make ourselves available to God for use based on His direction and not on our need to be important. Our ministry (though it does bring a reward) neither adds nor subtracts from our identity. This is a huge liberation. Our service becomes not a matter of compulsion but an expression of love.

MINISTRY – THE HERITAGE OF EVERY BELIEVER

Spiritual service and ministry is not confined to a chosen few but is the privilege and obligation of every supernaturally empowered believer. Centuries of tradition have stolen the spiritual ministry from the majority of believers. Today the Holy Spirit is reversing this. He wants every believer to cultivate not only the habit of humble practical service but of humble supernatural service as well.

All effective disciples look for opportunities to "heal the sick, raise the dead, cast out demons" share good news, win souls, and bring the comfort and the hope of the gospel to people.

The leadership ministries will always be necessary and relevant. Their task, however, is not primarily to do the ministry themselves but to equip, empower and train all believers for the supernatural acts of service. The leadership ministry is to *"equip the saints for the work of the ministry"* (Eph. 4:12),

147

"teaching them to observe all that I have asked you to do." (Mt. 28:20)

In this way, the whole company of millions of believers throughout the world will be released as a great team to bring the saving benefits of the Messiah Jesus to others. As believers lay hold of these realities a revolution is taking place in the face of Christianity.

The church is ceasing to be a group of mostly spectators being served by the pulpit ministry. Instead it is becoming - what it was always intended to be - a dynamic organism of enthusiastic and equipped believers who serve the world by bringing the blessing and benefits of God's redemption with them wherever they go. The sleeping giant of the church is now awakening from the binding cloths of religious tradition to become God's great army of love released in the world.

The supernaturally empowered believer is chosen not only to be the object of God's love and mercy but also to be a great blessing to the world around him. With this mind-set, life takes on a new purpose and meaning. Even the most menial act of service becomes charged with meaning and life when it is seen and done as an assignment from God. *"For whatever you do in word or deed, do it all for the glory of God."* (Col. 3:17) As we cultivate the habit of serving we will become the highly supernaturally empowered believers we were destined to be.

When the disciples of Jesus returned from their great mission of healing, preaching, expelling demons and liberating people, they were delighted with the effectiveness of the ministry. Jesus commended them but also corrected them: *"Do not rejoice that the demons are subject to you but that your names are written in heaven."* (Luke 10:20) Their worth was not to come from their work but from their position before Him as the adopted sons and daughters of God. Reward of ministry is not based on the size or impressiveness of the service but on its faithfulness.

THE BELIEVER LIVES TO SERVE

"For the Son of man also came not to be served but to serve, and to give his life as a ransom for many." (Mark 10:45) As Jesus came to serve and not to be served, we too are sent into the world from our ascended position to live in the earth as servants of God and of our fellow man. Jesus' service was not only for our benefit, but it was an example. *"If I then, your Lord and Teacher, have washed your feet, you also ought to wash one another's feet. For I have given you an example,*

that you also should do as I have done to you." (John 13:14-15)

> "I used to ask God to help me.
> Then I asked if I might help Him.
> I ended up by asking Him to
> do His work through me." - Hudson Taylor

Before we can serve, however, we must first allow the Lord to serve us. After He has served us and we have received His saving and transforming grace only then can we give ourselves to Him to use us to serve others.

Many want to serve the Lord without letting the Lord serve them first. We are not ready to serve Him and others through Him unless we allow Him to lift us up, cleanse and transform us and then send us.

We comfort and serve one another because we first have been helped ourselves. *"We love, because he first loved us."* (1 John 4:19) We do not serve because we think that we are superior to the ones we are serving. We serve because we know that we who serve today are as infinitely in need of service as the ones we serve.

THE HABIT OF SERVING/MINISTRY

It is a privilege to be able to serve and minister to others and there are as many varieties of service as there are people. We serve in natural ways and we also can serve in supernatural ways through the anointing of the Holy Spirit. It is common to call natural service 'work' and spiritual service 'ministry'. The scriptures make no such distinction: *"Whatever you do, do it all to the glory of God."* (1 Cor. 10:31)

> 'Why has God left us on the earth?
> Is it simply to be saved and sanctified? No it is to be at work in service to Him. Am I willing to be of no value to this age or this life except for one purpose and one alone – to be used to disciple men and women to the Lord Jesus.
> Christ. – Oswald Chambers

Natural service, such as nursing, washing feet, parenting, teaching, farming, manufacturing, cooking, cleaning, giving, encouraging and exhorting are equally vital areas of service. Believers can learn to function with equal joy in natural and spiritual service. We each have a different mixture of natural and spiritual service.

Both natural and spiritual service requires the development and cultivation of skills. Supernaturally empowered Believers should seek to excel in every area of service to which they are directed and should, therefore, also excel in acquiring the skills to make their acts of service most effectively. There is a tendency among some religious believers to regard education as somehow "worldly." It is true that it is 'worldly' to adopt the moral values of the unredeemed world .. but it is never "worldly" to acquire the best skills that can help us perform our service to others in the best way possible. Indeed, to pursue excellence in education for the motive of doing our job well is a deep expression of love.

DISTRACTED BY SERVICE

Service can become a dull grind when it is not seen in its context of love. The stressed worker who becomes so engrossed in the responsibility and pressure of work that he loses sight of its meaning gets lost in the treadmill of drudgery. On the other hand, when believers see work (however apparently insignificant) in the context of serving others it is transformed with purpose. It may not lose all its drudgery but it loses its meaninglessness.

In the famous gospel story when Martha was 'distracted by too much serving' she was like many today who are so stressed with the pressure of service that their work loses its meaning. Jesus praised Mary because she had chosen the better part. The better part is to serve in the context of love.

When we serve in love, the stress and pressure of our labors will not crowd out our joy in bringing help to the ones we love. In the words of Mike Bickle: "There are lovers and there are workers, and lovers get more work done than workers."

A family reunion where we celebrate with a special meal can be a wonderful celebration of love. It is easy for the labor of house cleaning and the stress of preparing a festive meal to overshadow the celebration of reunion. Martha, in the stress of getting everything ready for her VIP guest, lost sight of the fact that the purpose of the meal preparation was to enjoy the Master's company. For her the work overshadowed the purpose and she almost missed the enjoyment of the Master's visit. She lost sight of the main purpose of the work.

For the supernaturally empowered believer work is never mere drudgery – it is an assignment from God. Our service, however humble, takes on a fuller meaning when it is seen in this perspective - an assignment from God. *"So, whether you eat or drink, or whatever you do, do all to the glory of God."* (1 Corinthians 10:31) It is not the visible significance of our work that gives it its value.

WORKING WITH HIM AS FRIENDS

"No longer do I call you servants, for the servant does not know what his master does. But I have called you friends, for all things I have heard from My Father I have made known to you. You have not chosen Me, but I have chosen you and ordained you that you should go and bring forth fruit, and that your fruit should remain; that whatever you shall ask of the Father in My name, He may give it to you." (John 15:15-16)

Our assignments are not simply like assignments an army officer would pass on to his soldiers. Jesus calls us friends and not just servants. He is interested in partnering with us so that our acts of service become the fruit of our union with Him.

CHAPTER 8

THE HABIT OF
HEAVENLY LOVE

For the supernaturally empowered believer love is more than a habit - it is the atmosphere in which he lives. It is the amniotic fluid within which he thrives and outside of which he dies.

The believer in Jesus is empowered with an inflow of divine love that equips him for a whole new dimension and quality of living. When we are separated from this heavenly substance we live and behave abnormally. As fish were made for the sea and birds for the air, we were made to live in the atmosphere of God's love. *"And we have known and believed the love that God has in us. God is love and the one who lives in love lives in God and God lives in Him."* (1 John 4:16) When we do not remain in love we are like fish out of water and begin to stink – until we get back in again!

We are the only creatures on earth with a capacity to commune with God. In fact this defines who we are. That is why God gave us two great commandments, which sum up all the others:

"You shall love the Lord your God with all your heart, with all your mind, with all your soul, with all your strength." (Deut. 6:5)

"You shall love your neighbor as yourself." (Leviticus 19:18)

These words are not only words of command – they are words of prophecy. They are words of command because they illustrate what God requires of us. They are words of prophecy because they describe the way we shall be when the Spirit of love comes into us.

> "Tell me whom you love,
> and I will tell you what you are."
> - Arsene Houssaye

When we become reconciled with God, through the Atoning work of Jesus, the Holy Spirit pours this heavenly love into our hearts and we begin to experience God's love. This causes us to fall in love with Him, even though we cannot see Him. Relationship with God is no longer just a command - it is now an experiential reality.

"Therefore being justified by faith, we have peace with God through our Lord Jesus Christ. Through Him we also have access by faith into this

grace in which we stand, and we rejoice on the hope of the glory of God .... because the love of God has been poured out in our hearts through the Holy Spirit given to us." (Romans 5:1,2,5)

Through this heavenly imported love we are empowered to fulfill the two great commandments, to love God and love our neighbor. Jesus said, *"On these two commandments hang all the law and the prophets."* (Matthew 22:40) All else is trimming.

IT'S NOT NATURAL IT'S SUPERNATURAL!

Heavenly love, which the New Testament calls 'agape' and which the translators translate as 'love', is not a human kind of love. It is an attribute of God Himself which natural man is incapable of manifesting on his own. It is a direct import from heaven. It is part of the substance of God, which He transmits to us through the Holy Spirit, and it produces within us the benign attitude of wanting and doing the best for everyone. It is the great secret of the supernaturally empowered believer and the great key of the New Covenant.

Jeremiah and the prophets saw this coming reality, which the Messiah was to release into the earth. *"Behold, the days come, says the LORD, that I will cut a new covenant with the house of Israel, and with the house of*

Judah, not according to the covenant that I cut with their fathers in the day I took them by the hand to bring them out of the land of Egypt; which covenant of Mine they broke, although I was a husband to them, says the LORD; but this shall be the covenant that I will cut with the house of Israel: After those days, says the LORD, I will put My law in their inward parts, and write it in their hearts; and I will be their God, and they shall be My people. And they shall no more teach each man his neighbor and each man his brother, saying, Know the LORD; for they shall all know me, from the least of them to the greatest of them, says the LORD. For I will forgive their iniquity, and I will remember their sins no more." (Jer. 31:31-34)

The old laws of do's, don'ts and religious ordinances failed not because they were not good laws but because we were not good through the corruption of sin.

The New Covenant, inaugurated by Jesus, solves this problem. Through His atonement, God provides for the remission of sins and, through the gift of The Holy Spirit, He implants His love and righteousness within the hearts of believers. With the presence of God's Spirit within we are now equipped to fulfill the love commandment and to live as God designed us to live.

The breakthrough of the New Covenant is this:

1. God Himself in Jesus takes on Himself our guilt and shame, and

2. God Himself provides the love with which we can love Him and love one another.

LOVE IN THREE DIMENSIONS

As this heavenly love is downloaded into our hearts on a daily basis through the Holy Spirit, we live in the bright sunshine of God's love. This love is:

- love from God for God

- love from God for ourselves, and

- love from God for others.

It is a pipeline from heaven to us and through us. As we develop the habit of receiving and giving this love we become part of God's irrigation system of bringing heaven's goodness into our world. Keeping God's love flowing into and out of our hearts is our main responsibility and our greatest joy. *"Keep yourselves in the love of God, eagerly awaiting the mercy of our Lord Jesus Christ to everlasting life."* (Jude 1:21)

ENEMY-LOVING LOVE

"But I say to you who hear: Love your

enemies, do good to those who hate you." (Lk 6:27)

Heavenly love (agape) is not based on how others treat us. Neither is it a response to the attractiveness or goodness of others. It truly is heavenly. It empowers us to love the unlovely, the hateful and even our enemies. It equips us for enemy-loving love.

This kind of love is revolutionary in the best sense. When we love our enemies we can cross through barriers of ethnicity, culture, class and religion. Divisions created by historical enmities melt in the presence of this love. The supernaturally empowered believer can 'step out in love' to build a bridge of love to enemies.

In the 1970's Northern Ireland was being torn apart by sectarian hatred and violence. During this time our friend Cecil Kerr (while working as a pastor of a Protestant church in Enniskillen, Northern Ireland) was inspired by heavenly love to cross the sectarian barrier between him and his Catholic neighbors. He refused to conform or be held in by invisible walls of prejudice and determined to overcome them.

He did not agree with every theological or political view of his Catholic neighbors but he owed it to God and to Himself to love them. As he walked to the 'Catholic' side of the town he felt as if he could hear the voice of his ancestors crying: "Traitor! Traitor! Traitor!" This of course was not the voice of his ancestors but the voice of evil spirits of division that heavenly love within Him was confronting and overcoming.

By crossing the invisible divide in his town he overcame the spiritual forces of hostility that divided his society. In the process he broke through to a fuller Christian experience. He did not change his theological opinions but he became an instrument of God's love to his fellow Irish people. He along with many others walked through walls of hostility and created bridges of love that made way for a new society in Ireland.

Similar breakthroughs take place every day around the world. Supernaturally empowered believers build bridges of love that heal communities, repair relationships and transform society in a way that the political and justice systems could never do.

As we exercise and develop the habit of responding to heavenly love we overcome the barrier of racism, bigotry, class and religion and make breakthroughs for the love of God and the kingdom of God throughout the world. Believers who develop this habit are the greatest agents uplifting social change at every level on the earth today.

Heavenly Love Causes Us To Empty Ourselves

Jesus, *"though he was in the form of God, did not count equality with God a thing to be grasped, but emptied himself, taking the form of a servant, being born in the likeness of men. And being found in human form he humbled himself and became obedient unto death, even death on a cross."* (Philippians 2:6-8)

The supernaturally empowered believer follows the example of Jesus by learning to empty Himself in obedience to God and in the service of others. *"No one has greater love than this, that a man lay down his life for his friends."* (John 15:13)

Heavenly Love is self-empting, self-giving love. It is a motivating power that leads us to empty ourselves of our own interests in the pursuit of God's interests in others.

In fact, all supernaturally empowered believers are empowered for this kind of self-emptying love. This love inspires all of us in the interests of each of us and each of us in the interests of all of us. It transforms all relationships and fills them with meaning and worth. When Christian doctors and nurses empty themselves in the interests of their patients, pastors in the interests of their congregations, parents in the interests of their children, employers in the interests of their employees, employees in the interests of their employers, life is lit up by the Son light of heavenly love.

When Heavenly Love takes over his heart, the supernaturally empowered believer sees life in a whole new way. His motivation changes, and instead of asking "How can I get the most out of life?" he asks "How can I give my life away in the service of the One who loves me?" His life escapes from the tight walls of self-centeredness and he begins to be less interested in merely his own survival and more interested in lifting others up.

Paul describes this kind of love when he writes: *"And I will very gladly spend and be spent for your souls, even if loving you more and more, I am loved the less."* (2 Cor. 12:15)

> ## While faith makes all things possible, love makes all things easy.
> ### – Evan Hopkins

As Jesus says: *"He who loves his life must lose it and he who loses his life finds it."* (Mark 8:35) This is not a call to self-mutilation or self-repression but an exhortation to come fully alive by escaping the prison house of self-centeredness and losing ourselves in the river of His love for others.

It is only when we discover this self-empting love that we reach our fullest godliness and deepest humanness as supernaturally empowered believers.

CHAPTER 9

THE HABIT OF ASSEMBLY

"*And let us consider how to stir up one another to love and good works, not neglecting to meet together, as is the habit of some, but encouraging one another, and all the more as you see the Day drawing near.*" (Heb. 10:24-25)

CHRISTIANITY IS PERSONAL & CORPORATE

Each one makes his way individually into the kingdom of God by personally accepting the gift of eternal life and by personally repenting.

As we relate to God through Jesus, the Messiah, we become spiritually and vitally connected to a great worldwide community of believers made up of people of every nation and culture. As part of this amazing community of believers, saved by grace, transformed by the Spirit, instructed by the Word of God, we are commissioned to serve and advance the kingdom of God throughout the earth.

We cannot live our Christian lives alone, nor can we fulfill this great commission alone. We live it out in partnership with this vast company. Our lives as believers are both personal and corporate.

Though our relationship with God is personal, we share a common task as heirs together of His grace and enjoying a common commission and commandment. We all need and complete each other. We each take our part in this great team of love and mercy, through which God reaches compassionately into this world.

"For just as the body is one and has many members, and all the members of the body, though many, are one body, so it is with Christ. For by one Spirit we were all baptized into one body - Jews or Greeks, slaves or free - and all were made to drink of one Spirit. For the body does not consist of one member but of many. If the foot should say, "Because I am not a hand, I do not belong to the body," that would not make it any less a part of the body. And if the ear should say, "Because I am not an eye, I do not belong to the body," that would not make it any less a part of the body. If the whole body were an eye, where would be the hearing? If the whole body were an ear, where would be the sense of smell? But as it is, God arranged the organs in the body, each one of them, as he chose.

If all were a single organ, where would the body be? As it is, there are many parts, yet one body. The eye cannot say to the hand, "I have no need of you," nor again the head to the feet, "I have no need of you." On the contrary, the parts of the body, which seem to be weaker, are indispensable, and those parts of the body, which we think less honorable, we invest with the greater honor, and our unpreventable parts are treated with greater modesty, which our more presentable parts do not require. But God has so composed the body, giving the greater honor to the inferior part, that there may be no discord in the body, but that the members may have the same care for one another. If one member suffers, all suffer together; if one member is honored, all rejoice together. Now you are the body of Christ and individually members of it." (1 Cor. 12:12-27)

At the basis of Christianity is the commandment to love one another as Jesus has loved us (John 13:34). Love cannot be lived in a vacuum. Neither can we serve the common mission of the Body of Christ by being isolated from the rest of the Body.

PRIVATE PRACTICE OF FAITH IS NOT ENOUGH

Many believers do not participate in the common mission of the church. They keep in touch with God through their private prayer, study and devotion but do not see the necessity of assembling with other believers. When they remain apart, they miss out on the stream of edification and inspiration that comes through the whole Body of Christ. Conversely, as they refrain from meeting together with other believers, their absence creates a vacant place at the table, and the whole company is diminished by their absence.   God   is constantly pouring fresh streams of vision, life and inspiration into His Body. *"His mercies are new every morning."* (Lam. 3:23) Those who isolate themselves from this miss out on the fresh strength that God is giving to His Body.

> "You shall not see my face unless your brother is with you"- Genesis 43.5

Some do this out of a mistaken idea that God has said everything He is going to say and done everything He is going to do.

God has set things up so that not all of our growth in grace and receiving of His benefits will come to us through our personal devotions. He has arranged that much of our growth and building up in grace should come through other members of His Body.

"... speaking truth in love, we may grow up in all things into him, who is the head, even Christ; from whom all the body fitly framed and knit together through that which every joint supplies according to the working in due measure of each several part, makes the increase of the body unto the building up of itself in love." (Eph. 4:15-16)

SOLITUDE ALIGNS WITH GOD

At times it is necessary to withdraw from the corporate side of the Body of Christ to seek the Lord privately, intimately and personally. At such times we can reassess our place in Him and our place with the rest of the Body.

However, such times of withdrawal should only be for a season. We should re-enter to fulfill our place within Christ's Body.

However, without seasons of solitude we can lose sight of our own identity and calling. We can get so caught up in church programs and activity that we can lose the sense of our own uniqueness and mission. Without withdrawing from the many voices around us we will miss the voice of God to us. Jesus is our great example. He often withdrew from the crowds to avoid being caught up in man's agenda and to hear the Father's voice. He was careful not to become entangled in the religious 'parties' of His time, the humanistic Sadducees, the tradition bound Pharisees and the politicized Herodians. Instead, He withdrew from men's religious factions so that He could relate to the needs of the world on God's terms and not on man's. Jesus often withdrew from human company to get alone with God, most notably at the commencement of His ministry to examine His motivations and to overcome temptation.

The greatest supernaturally empowered believers withdraw to examine what is in their heart in solitude before God. This is where they receive direction and guidance from Him.

JESUS INVITES US TO COME ASIDE

"And He said to them, Come aside into a deserted place and rest a little. For there were many coming and going, and they had no opportunity even to eat. And they departed by boat into a deserted place." (Mark 6: 31-32)

Jesus seeing that, because of pressure, His disciples had no opportunity to eat, called them aside. All who want to be effective followers of His will develop the habit of time apart with Him for personal spiritual nourishment.

Pastor Sunday Adele, pastor of one of the largest churches in Europe in Kiev, Ukraine, takes a week off each month to seek the Lord.

For the first two days, he meditates on the phrase: "Lord you are God and I am not."

The next two days, he keeps on asking, "Lord show me what You are doing on the earth today."

The last three days, he keeps on asking "Lord show me my part in what You are doing on the earth today."

FROM SOLITUDE TO COMMUNITY

Times of solitude, however, should always end with a return to the community. *"And Jesus returned in the power of the Spirit into Galilee. And a report went out throughout all the neighborhood concerning Him."* (Luke 4:14)

Times apart are vital but if we remain isolated He cannot lead us into our place and function within the Body. The believer is like a coal that is part of the great fire of God's love on the earth. When you remove the individual coal from the fire the flame dies.

We personally and individually relate to God and then He relates us to the best place for us in His church. It is the Spirit that leads and relates us. Though we are strengthened, inspired and used within the church, we each remain responsible for our own personal choices and obedience to God and His way. The community is not a mediator between the believer and God. He must relate and connect with God personally and then receive fellowship, guidance, instruction, love and inspiration in the community.

God will meet us alone but He also meets us in community. It was when they were all together in one accord on the day of Pentecost that God visited the believers with the outpouring of the Holy Spirit (Acts 2). The children of Israel journeyed from Egypt to Canaan as a team and together they experienced the miraculous working of God. As well as receiving from the Lord privately and individually we are to partake of the corporate mission, anointing and blessing of the entire Christian community.

Sometimes the community goes beyond its parameters of instructing, equipping, encouraging, loving and training its members, to controlling and domineering them. God sets us in the Body - it is NOT the Body that sets us in God. The balance of direct relationship and corporate edification, personal experience and team work must always be maintained.

When this balance is lost the community becomes oppressive to the believer's liberty and function. When the believer becomes isolated the strengthening of the Body is forfeited.

ONE CHURCH, MANY CONGREGATIONS

The Body of Christ (there is only one church) consists not only of millions of members but also countless organizations and congregations. Some believers emphasize a certain aspect of Christian truth and some another. Sectarianism causes congregations to be isolated from each other in religious ghettos and separated from the fresh life and inspiration that comes from different parts of the body.

Not only is the Body composed of many parts - it is composed of clusters of parts. One congregation or denomination is not the whole church and, therefore, to isolate one congregation from the inspiration of the rest of the body causes great weakness. Congregations need to support and strengthen each other.

In our effort to be contemporary we can sometimes cut ourselves off from the wisdom, richness and lessons of previous generations. The supernaturally empowered believer knows how to draw from the experience of all generations of believers without getting enmeshed in traditions that "make void the Word of God."

"And he said to them, "Therefore every scribe who has been trained for the kingdom of heaven is like a householder who brings out of his treasure what is new and what is old." (Matt. 13:52)

Jesus, when He spoke to John as recorded in the Book of Revelation, showed that He was aware of the weakness of each local congregation but pointed out that the most supernaturally empowered believers whom He called 'the overcomers' would not be limited by the weakness of their local congregation but would transcend those limitations to enter into the fullness of kingdom living.

Let us practice this habit of assembling together for maximum blessing!

CHAPTER 10

THE HABIT OF REST

The lion, the king of the beasts, rests about 20 hours a day. Rest is an essential part of life.

Contemporary life is designed to get maximum production from human beings. Our identity gets lost in the machine of production. Sabbath Rest is the sign that we are not slaves but sons.

Rest is not just a pause between work periods but also a time of return to our source, recovery of identity and celebration of God's goodness. *"For thus said the Lord GOD, the Holy One of Israel, in returning and rest you shall be saved; in quietness and in trust shall be your strength. And you would not."* (Isaiah 30:15)

God placed the need of rest into our bodies and lives. This need for rest is not a weakness but part of the rhythm of our lives.

Thomas Edison thought that sleep was a waste of time and a mere biological necessity. The light bulb has given us a 24-hour day where life never stops. In the midst of this twenty-four hour day world it is vital that we not be sucked into the drivenness and spirit of the age, and stay in rhythm with the pace of God.

It is one thing to embrace technological advances but it is another matter that our whole rhythm of live is manipulated by the world system.

Milton described God as his "Great Taskmaster" but God is not a tyrannical taskmaster. He is a loving Father who wants us to be fulfilled and fruitful, as we discover a pace of life and production that is in perfect harmony with Him. God looks at us as friends and as children and not just as producers. Without rest we cannot reflect and we will become enveloped in the agenda and pace of the world.

The opposite of rest is stress. Stress and lack of rest are leading sources of ill health in people today. Supernaturally empowered believers combat not only the fact of stress but also the spirit of stress.

To fail to rest is to weaken 'the goose that lays the golden egg'. In our greed for more production we often do not care sufficiently for ourselves. Neglect of the body and of rest may look spiritual but in fact is a violation of the laws of the kingdom of God.

THE PAUSE BUTTON

God revealed the necessity of rest in the first chapter of Genesis. He Himself rested – not because He was tired - but because He needed to enjoy and savor what was accomplished in the week.

In the wilderness before the codified Law of Sinai was given, God taught the Israelis the principle of rest and showed them that they would not receive any more by working on the Sabbath. It is not how much we work that makes us productive but how smart we work. As we pause we can be redirected by God and receive fresh ideas and direction.

The fact that we are not bound in a legalistic way to the Sabbath does not mean that the principle of rest, which is a universal law of life, should not be respected. All the most supernaturally empowered believers know how to take rest. Jesus asks us to come to Him and receive rest. *"Come to me, all who labor and are heavy laden, and I will give you rest. Take my yoke upon you, and learn from me; for I am gentle and lowly in heart, and you will find rest for your souls. For my yoke is easy, and my burden is light."* (Matt 11:28-30)

THE GREATER SABBATH REST

There is a greater rest for the believer than simply the spiritual, mental and physical rest of a

177

day free from labor. This is a rest which religious observance could never give the Jews or any other. Religion can never give the rest that Jesus brings. *"For if Joshua had given them rest, God would not speak later of another day. So then, there remains a Sabbath rest for the people of God; for whoever enters God's rest also ceases from his labors as God did from his. Let us therefore strive to enter that rest, that no one fall by the same sort of disobedience."* (Hebr. 4:1-11)

Here the scriptures speak of the rest of the believer who has discovered and entered the kingdom of God. We rest from our works and rest on God's work.

We rest on the redemption provided for us by Jesus. We rest in the fact that (though we are not yet perfect) we are perfectly accepted and loved through the work of Jesus on the cross. Our sins are perfectly atoned for and we are reconciled to God. We rest in God's redemption through the work of Jesus. We rest in His provision. We rest in His promises.

In addition, as we cease from our works, we loose ourselves from the false burden of self, of the world, of religion, and we take the 'light' yoke of the Lord. We receive work to do from Him for which we are perfectly suitable. Religion is a taskmaster and the agenda of the world gives no rest. But when we cease living for self and from self we find the agenda of the Lord and our works proceed from His instructions.

When we cease from our works we do not cease from work. We cease from empty work and dead work. We work not for our salvation but we work as saved people to bless the world around us with our work as God directs.

The key to the supernaturally empowered believer's rest is to rest in faith on the finished work of the cross and then to take the yoke of the Lord upon himself.

THE VINE & THE BRANCHES

The greatest metaphor for the special rest of the believer is Jesus' allegory of the vine and the branches. *"I am the vine, you are the branches. He who abides in me, and I in him, he it is that bears much fruit, for apart from me you can do nothing."* (John 15:5)

The little twig rests on the vine and as it rests there it drinks up the sap of the vine and passes it on to the developing fruit at the end of the branch. It is fruitful while resting and working from rest. It is bound to a certain task and, as it rests in its place and task, it produces beautiful fruit.

The most supernaturally empowered believers have rested from their own drivenness and the pressures of the world. They are available and useful in the work the Master gives them and are, therefore, the most effective disciples of all.

A Prayer To Receive Jesus As Savior,
To Forgive Others & To Live By God's Ways

Father, God I come to You just as I am. I acknowledge I am a sinner and have sinned and cannot save myself. I believe that, on the Cross Your Son, Jesus took the blame, shame, judgment and atoned for these sins, so that I could be forgiven, reconciled to You and receive a new nature.

Father, I accept Your forgiveness, and I in return forgive all for whatever wrong they have done against me. Take all bitterness, anger and selfishness out of my heart .I ask You, Jesus to come into my heart and make me a new creation. Fill me with Your Spirit by replacing my sinful nature with Your life. Empower me by Your Spirit to live a life of love, righteousness, peace and joy. Live in me and love through me. I give my self to You, Lord Jesus, and put my life under Your protection.

I commit myself to seek Your ways and to walk in them by the supernatural power of the Holy Spirit. I declare and believe that my sins are forgiven, that You are my Lord and Savior, and that Your Spirit has liberated me from the penalty and power of sin and that now I am a new creature in You. You live in me and I live in You. Amen

(Read: Isaiah 53:4-6: Romans 10:9-10. John 3:16; 2 Corinthians 5:17-21 and tell others that Jesus is now your Lord and Savior.)

To order more copies of

The Supernatural Habits
of the
Spirit Empowered Believer

write to:

Reconciliation Outreach
P.O. Box 2778
Stuart, FL 34995

or e-mail paulandnuala@comcast.net
or by going on line to:
www.reconciliationoutreach.net

You can help us spread this good news by making sure that your local Christian bookstore carries this book and other books by Paul & Nuala O'Higgins.

Books by Paul & Nuala O'Higgins:

Christianity Without Religion

The Supernatural Habits of the
Spirit Empowered Believer

Good News in Israel's Feasts

New Testament Believers & The Law

The Four Great Covenants

In Israel Today With Yeshua

The Blessed Hope

Removing The Tares - The Time Of The Harvest

Have You Received The Holy Spirit?

Life-Changing, World-Changing Prayer.

Salvation Of Spirit, Soul & Body

ABOUT THE AUTHORS

Paul and Nuala O'Higgins are natives of Ireland who reside in Stuart, Florida. They are the directors of Reconciliation Outreach – a ministry of teaching and interdenominational evangelism wich has taken them to more than 30 nations

In full-time ministry together since 1977 they have ministered in over thirty nations. Nuala's degree is in Education and Paul's degrees are in Philosophy and Theology. Paul also holds a doctorate in Biblical Theology.

They are heralds of the love of God made available by the Cross. Their call is to make known the treasures of God's kingdom and equip believers to be effective followers of Jesus, and to embrace the full potential of their inheritance in Him.

Made in the USA
Columbia, SC
05 September 2018